Discovering Nonviolence

Charles E. Collyer and Ira G. Zepp, Jr.

TryForFurther Books

This book is a portion of
Nonviolence: Origins and Outcomes, 3rd edition,
by Charles E. Collyer and Ira G. Zepp, Jr.,
Foreword by Bernard LaFayette, Jr.

Nonviolence: Origins and Outcomes, 3rd ed.
Part 1 - *Discovering Nonviolence*
Part 2 - *Agape and Ahimsa: Twin Roots of Nonviolence*

Cover Painting "Mudfork Falls, Sky Valley, NC" by Ellen
Elmes.
Image prepared by Don Elmes

Dedications

For John Lidgey, 1948 - 2001, my friend of 50 years,
who was intensely interested in nonviolent change.
In grateful memory,
- Charlie

For Montgomery J. Shroyer - Biblical scholar,
social activist, nonviolence teacher.
With gratitude and respect.
- Ira

Acknowledgments

I will always be grateful for the opportunity to work with Ira Zepp during the last decade of his life. Ira had a way of being both reassuring and challenging at the same time – what a friend! As we explored the overlap between his field of religious studies and mine, psychology, I experienced both the joy of an interdisciplinary collaboration and the vertigo of stepping out into unknown territory. In the end, he became a pretty good psychologist, and I came to appreciate the insights into nonviolence that have arisen in many of the world's religions and in the thinking of many theologians.

As always, I thank my wife and partner Pam Zappardino, who first introduced me to her mentor Ira Zepp many years ago, and who continues to guide our work together through the Ira and Mary Zepp Center for Nonviolence and Peace Education.

I also thank the people of Common Ground on the Hill, Silver Oak Academy, Shepherd's Staff, NAACP Branch 7014, and all the other members of my community who provide me every day with nonviolent discoveries and wonderful examples of *agape* and *ahimsa* in practice.

Charles E. Collyer
Carroll County, Maryland, 2017

CONTENTS

Preface to the Third Edition

The late Dr. Zepp and I have been gratified by how our students and friends have responded to the first two editions of *Nonviolence: Origins and Outcomes*. The book has been read as a text in courses and discussed in book clubs, and has even been reported useful as affirmation and inspiration, although that goes a bit beyond its original purpose.

Nonviolence: Origins and Outcomes grew out of my experiences as a teacher of psychology and Dr. Zepp's as a teacher of religious studies and theology. Each of us in our own way was learning how to teach about nonviolence, a subject that both of us felt must be "brought down to earth" if its lessons were ever to take strong root.

The first edition, published in 2003, was written with the events of September 11, 2001 fresh in our minds. The second edition (2007) made the book more widely available beyond the United States and India, as the use of the book in schools and colleges began to grow. In this third edition, the entire book has been revised and updated, it has been split into two volumes, titled *Discovering Nonviolence* and *Agape and Ahimsa*, and it has migrated to electronic form. *Discovering Nonviolence* (comprising five of the original chapters) is an introduction to nonviolence, viewed as a comprehensive moral and practical framework for solving problems. *Agape and Ahimsa* (comprising four of the original chapters), represents Ira Zepp's thoughtful analysis of the philosophical and religious roots of nonviolence, including a dialogue with Bill Holmes about pacifism.

Two chapters are also available as separate ebooks. The first, *What Goes on in a Nonviolence Training*, will be of interest to trainers and teachers of nonviolence, and to intermediate and advanced students. The second, *There's More to Nonviolence Than I Thought,* amplifies the commonplace saying that nonviolence is active rather than passive, by discussing several specific ways in which a person may be changed when considering nonviolence more deeply.

Charles E. Collyer
Carroll County, Maryland, 2017

Foreword to *Nonviolence: Origins and Outcomes*

The past century has brought humankind into an era of mass destruction, one where our ability to produce massive suffering seems to have raced ahead of our capacity to demonstrate compassion for one another. We must search for paths into the future that will turn away from destructive goals and strategies, paths that will reject violence as a way to solve problems. If we are to rise to a new level, it will be necessary for us to re-examine basic concepts, re-draw our roadmap, re-direct our footsteps, and re-shape our vision for the future.

This book by Charles Collyer and Ira Zepp makes a significant contribution to the field of nonviolence and peace studies. The experience of the authors as teachers of nonviolence, and the depth of their commitment to nonviolent social change, is evident in every chapter. Many scholars and practitioners will benefit greatly from this work, particularly those who have recently come into this field of study and are developing their own skills as teachers of peace. This book lays out a foundation of *ahimsa*, *agape* love, and achievable nonviolence that belongs in the forefront of the 21st century's search for a new way.

Dr. Bernard LaFayette, Jr.

Prologue – An Unexpected Assignment

It was mid-January, the beginning of a Spring semester at the University of Rhode Island. I was then Chair of the Psychology Department, and the instructor for a group of first-year graduate students in the department's orientation seminar. These students were impressive. All had come to the university with strong credentials. They displayed an obvious enthusiasm for learning more about Psychology, and held high expectations of their program faculty. Most were in their mid-twenties to mid-thirties, some coming directly from bachelor's degree programs and some from the working world. They were not kids, but grown men and women with at least a semester of graduate work under their belts, well-educated and pretty sophisticated.

The roster consisted of about twenty students from our three program tracks - Clinical, Experimental, and School Psychology, all mixed together. This integration was more the exception than the rule in their courses, because for the most part the three programs functioned separately. In this seminar, however, the students were getting to know each other during their first year, and learning about the department's faculty, its research resources, and the current state of the field of Psychology.

We were meeting on a Monday. The Martin Luther King Jr. Holiday was coming up the following week, so our second seminar meeting of the new semester would be in two weeks' time, and I made an announcement to that effect. Then, having mentioned the holiday, I happened to ask how many people had ever read Dr. King's *Letter from Birmingham Jail*. No one raised a hand.

I had become a nonviolence trainer about two years before. In that role, I had often assigned the *Letter* and led discussions on it. But my nonviolence workshops usually consisted of younger students or members of community groups. I had never assigned King's *Letter* to graduate students in Psychology.

Still, I was surprised that no one in this well-educated group had read the *Letter from Birmingham Jail*. I asked how many people had ever read anything by Dr. King. Only a couple of hands were raised. One person related that when she was in high school, her class had spent a day learning about the Civil Rights Movement. She knew Dr. King mainly for his "I Have a Dream" speech, which she remembered reading. She was hazy on the details of what had happened during the Movement. She had heard that I was involved in nonviolence training, and that the curriculum I used was derived from King and Gandhi. She reflected that that her brief high school exposure to the Civil Rights Movement had not included a discussion of nonviolence, or King's relationship to it.

I decided that this was one of those "teachable moments" when a gap has been acknowledged and the next step would be to fill it in. I said something like this: "Well, I'm going to give you an assignment. Go out and find something to read by Dr. King. It can be the *Letter from Birmingham Jail*, or anything else. When we get back together in two weeks, we can talk about what you found. I'm especially interested in what you think about King as a psychologist." (Without meaning to, I left open the question whether "as a psychologist" meant "the psychologist," placing King in the role, or "from a psychological viewpoint," inviting the student to be the psychologist. Consequently, some people interpreted the assignment one way, and some the other way.)

That homework assignment turned out to be one of the most successful I have ever given to a group of students, at any level. When the class met again two weeks later, almost all were genuinely excited about King and nonviolence and civil rights and the psychology of it all. They had located and read King's *Letter*, and many other books, sermons, and essays. Several expressed amazement that they had not known of King as a thinker and writer before this. Some had decided to participate in one of the King holiday events because of the assignment. The students were full of admiration for King's moral approach to difficult conflicts, for his ability to respect and even care for his adversaries, for his skill as a coalition-builder. And they were fascinated by the dynamics of nonviolence, by its counterintuitive yet very natural quality, and by its power at times to cut through human problems and provide surprising solutions. The relevance of nonviolence for psychology, and vice versa, just leapt out at them. One student asked, quite early in our discussion, "Why didn't I ever have a course on this?" Indeed.

On that day I began to wonder why Psychology and the traditions of nonviolence were not in closer touch with each other. Because the historical origins of nonviolence lay outside the relatively young field of Psychology, in other disciplines such as religion, politics, and literature, and in social problems outside the academy, it was understandable that the topic had not made its way into the standard curricula of Psychology programs. But the impact of nonviolence in practice, and its influence on people's thinking and emotions, loudly say "psychology" to me, and I have come to believe that a stronger bridge needs to be built between the two domains.

Nonviolence grew originally from religious roots. Psychology is a secular, not a religious, field of study. Yet many psychologists readily acknowledge that some "spiritual" understanding of life is important to them, and that though they find spirituality largely missing from the mainstream of their field, they feel it is an important element in their own work and in understanding human nature. Martin Luther King, Jr. And Mahatma Gandhi before him, each crafted a practical social vision of his religion, combining a positive, spiritually satisfying view of humankind with political energy for progress toward freedom and justice. Psychologists join with many other

14

audiences in finding that such a combination of spirituality and practicality fills a void for them.

This book has been written to whet an appetite for nonviolence in as many readers as possible. We think it will appeal to both students of "official" Psychology, and to people interested in everyday psychology who also have an interest in spiritual and social values. More generally, we believe that nonviolence offers "common ground" where religious and secular concerns can intersect, and where bridges can be built between cultures, disciplines, and factions of many kinds. We have seen the study and practice of nonviolence reap rich and creative rewards, and so wish to encourage as many people as possible to explore this common ground, to begin the building and crossing of these bridges.

Chapter 1 - Discovering Nonviolence

Before digging into the stories and the conceptual richness of nonviolence, most potential students of the topic seem to hold a stereotype about it - a set of four beliefs that, by default, capture the meaning of the word "nonviolence" for them. First is the belief that nonviolence is a passive philosophical approach in which events are just allowed to happen without any intervention or interference. Second, a person may associate nonviolence with cowardice, and violence with courage. Third is the idea that nonviolence is just being nice to people. And fourth is the view of nonviolence as being easy, as being the path of least resistance in many of life's challenging situations.

A little study soon shows that nonviolence is the very opposite in every respect. It involves active problem solving rather than passive acquiescence. It very often requires awesome courage in the face of real threats and terrible fear. It is likely to demand difficult confrontations, and intense discomfort both for the just and the unjust. And it has therefore been the more difficult path, the road less traveled, in almost all of its most famous examples. These contrasts, and others, help to explain why the discovery of nonviolence very often involves a series of surprises for the new student.

Why does the old stereotype of nonviolence persist? Many reasons could be given, but it seems to us that the understanding of nonviolence as passive, cowardly, "nice", and easy, is maintained by very strong psychological and cultural forces. Further, some of these forces are accepted and familiar, but upon reflection just don't make sense. Others are hard to perceive, much less to challenge. We will discuss some of these forces in this chapter and throughout the book.

Despite these forces, nonviolence continues to be discovered, and rediscovered, by people who need it. Throughout history, in many cultures all over the world, people have discovered the power of nonviolent motives, feelings, tactics, and values. Nonviolence has given direction to religions, enabled embattled peoples to survive, and achieved dramatic triumphs over injustice and violence.[1] However, the understanding of nonviolence as a powerful antidote to both violence and complacency is often lost, or submerged in a culture's repertoire of traditions, and so must be explicitly rediscovered again in response to a new set of problems.

Between rediscoveries, when people have slid into the acceptance and even glorification of violence, and when wealth and distance enable many people to evade basic human problems rather than solve them, the stereotyped view of nonviolence - passive, cowardly, nice, easy - prevails. The stereotype is abetted by the structure of the word nonviolence itself: "nonviolence" sounds like it should simply mean "not violent," a phrase with apparently obvious passive connotations.

Possessing this understanding of nonviolence, people paradoxically both approve of it and are frightened and confused by it. They endorse it as a remedy for the violence that frightens or annoys them, and are enthusiastic about its adoption – at least by others. However, they confidently "know" that they themselves could not stick with nonviolence if their own lives or family were threatened. They proclaim that nonviolence will not work in situations that have reached crisis proportions.

Well, to address the last point first, sometimes nonviolence has worked in crisis situations. But for some reason we do not tell stories about the courageous and successful use of nonviolence very often. Perhaps nonviolence is just as frightening to us as violence! Perhaps we believe that we will be made vulnerable if we embrace nonviolence, as if we were not already so. Perhaps we refrain from telling stories about nonviolence to protect ourselves, and our loved ones, from exposure to danger.

But what if telling stories of nonviolence were more likely to help us survive than to put us in danger? It would then be tragic if we did not tell these stories and try to learn from them. We will tell some of the stories of nonviolence in this book, and you can judge their value for yourself. Some of the stories are indeed about crisis situations, but many are about how crises can be prevented through a nonviolent approach to life and its problems.

Quitting Smoking and Learning to Swim

Here are two analogies that may capture the idea of nonviolence as a skill set or a life-long practice rather than a temporary tactic or momentary decision.

Quitting smoking is never seriously suggested as a cure for the person who is already dying of cancer. Rather, we understand that quitting, if done early enough, can reduce a person's risk of getting lung cancer in the first place. We would not test the value of "quitting smoking" by its failure to cure a terminally ill person. Yet nonviolence is often put to such a test, when it is finally tried as a form of eleventh-hour crisis intervention. Nonviolence is often deemed to have failed when, in a crisis, it does not magically make the threat of violence go away. This kind of test is unfair; it is like dismissing the value of quitting smoking because a critically ill recent quitter died anyway. Why would people reject nonviolence so unfairly? Perhaps this is one of the ways in which we human beings defend ourselves against the supposed dangers of adopting nonviolence. "See? We tried nonviolence, and it didn't work." (That is, it didn't magically overcome violence *right now*.) "So now, let's go back to our old habits."

A second meaningful comparison is to swimming. Learning nonviolence is very much like learning to swim. Like swimming, nonviolence is enriching, useful in everyday tasks, preventive of threats to life, and very helpful when threats nevertheless arise. Everyone understands the value of swimming lessons. However, not everyone understands the value, or has even heard of, systematic lessons in nonviolence. It is important to know that during the U.S. Civil Rights Movement and in other human rights movements around the world, nonviolence training was undertaken to prepare for predictable threats such as being beaten up or attacked by police dogs. Demonstrators in the campaigns where nonviolence was the guiding principle were not thrown unprepared into the sea of injustice and hostility, but received lessons ahead of time that taught them what to expect and how to respond. We will see later that it was their adherence to what they had learned in those lessons that made it possible for the movement to strike down legalized segregation.

The phrase "sink or swim" brings to mind the limited, frightening options of an unprepared person floundering in crisis. Sometimes this phrase is adopted literally, as a strategy for teaching someone how to swim; in that case it means plunging the student into deep water on the first day of the course. We leave to others the task of judging the merits and shortcomings of this approach to learning. However, we are pretty sure that mastery cannot be achieved in this way. That is, we are confident that regardless of how one was introduced to the water, it is best to take progressively more challenging lessons, get lots of practice, and master the skills of swimming well before a real crisis arises when floundering simply will not do. The same can be said for many other skills, including the skills of nonviolence.

If we are lucky, crises occupy only a small fraction of our lives. Nonviolence may or may not provide the solution during the 1% (say) of our days when we are in real crisis. But it certainly provides valuable guidance during the other 99%. In fact, it might be said that all the problems successfully solved in this larger portion of our time, are examples of nonviolence at work. Should we not study our own successes in order to learn how to have more of them? In this book, we will present nonviolence as something to practice not just when the threat of violence is about to overwhelm us, but all the time. We believe that this more comprehensive approach is in keeping with what Mahatma Gandhi and Martin Luther King Jr. meant by nonviolence.

The Meaning of Nonviolence

We have said that the old stereotype of nonviolence is mistaken, and that the structure of the word itself gives a wrong impression of what nonviolence means. Naturally enough, nonviolence does include opposition to violence. One of the origins of nonviolence discussed in our *Agape and Ahimsa: Twin Roots of Nonviolence*, is *ahimsa*, the Sanskrit word meaning non-injury, a vow not to commit violence in any way. Nonviolence also means valuing and caring about human beings, simply because they are people. Accordingly, the other root of nonviolence is *agape*, the Greek word for unconditional love toward others. In addition to these two roots, the meaning of nonviolence resides in the lives of people who are trying to

21

follow a nonviolent path, and in the nonviolent solutions they create to address life's problems. So for us, the meaning of nonviolence has come to include both its origins, *agape* and *ahimsa*, and its outcomes as expressed in nonviolent living and problem-solving.

As you can see, nonviolence for us is not a simple idea but many-faceted, not a single idea but a constellation of many. Throughout history, many versions of nonviolence have developed, some from religious traditions and some with more secular or combined roots. We adopt an inclusive "big tent" approach in which all of these versions are valued, and are seen as tending in the same general direction. We do not presume to speak for them all, but we will try to refrain from elevating one specific version over another. Can a general, "big tent" definition of nonviolence be given? Perhaps not to everyone's satisfaction, given this complicated picture, but here is an attempt:

Nonviolence is an approach to life in which people are valued for their own sake, and in which the idea of successful living includes peace achieved through peaceful means. It demands the best that people have to offer, both in crisis situations and in the course of everyday life. It is active, courageous, realistic, and challenging. It can be learned. Nonviolence does not have to be performed perfectly. But to the extent that it can be practiced, it makes a valuable contribution to the quality of life and to

relationships between people, whether they are friends or adversaries, by creating conditions that support human beings rather than doing violence to them.

Obstacles and Paradoxes

We hope that nonviolence sounds interesting and attractive so far. It has been so attractive to some of our students that they have asked us for advice on how to make a career out of teaching nonviolence. A few of them have actually done so. It turns out, however, that advocating for nonviolence on a large scale is quite difficult. For many people in society today, significant obstacles stand in the way of adopting nonviolence. In our opinion, there is a pressing need for more understanding of these barriers to nonviolence education and for more people who are willing to work on overcoming them. Here are just a few of the obstacles we have encountered in our work:

First, everyone in the world seems to believe that the world would be better off if only *everyone else* were less violent. Now, if everyone endorses nonviolence at least to this extent, why is the world still so violent? Clearly, we need to come to terms, not only with the violence of others, but also with our own. Ironically, most of us have a strong, even desperate, tendency to cling to violence as an option for ourselves, and to avoid serious consideration of living without this option.

Second, the wisdom of the ages regarding violence and the feelings associated with it, is sometimes not so wise. For example, the idea that anger must be cathartically "vented" is very widespread. In fact, many people believe that when angry, greater harm will come to them if they take some time to think about how to respond than if they act out their anger immediately. However, decades of research, less widely known, support the alternative views that (1) the perceived necessity of venting anger is just a compelling illusion, and (2) learning skills to deal with anger is more effective in almost every way. For a readable treatment of alternative theories of anger, see Carol Tavris's book *Anger: The Misunderstood Emotion*.[2]

Third, when the wisdom of the ages really is wise, we sometimes just don't get it. An example is the Golden Rule: Treat others as you want them to treat you. For the most part, this is a profoundly good, nonviolent insight.[3] Too often, however, we operate on what might be called the Rule of Payback: Treat others the way they have treated you. This rule is also expressed in the familiar saying: An eye for an eye and a tooth for a tooth. Some people apparently cannot distinguish between the Golden Rule and the Rule of Payback; they just don't get the difference. Justice is equated, not with fair and respectful treatment for all, but with getting revenge; and peace is equated, not with positive, constructive lives and relationships, but with simply being left alone.

Fourth, we human beings become adapted to unjust and destructive conditons all too readily. What is *familiar* to us

24

through long experience - even if the experience is ghastly - comes to feel *normal* through mere exposure and repetition. And violence is usually repetitive. Most of the violence in the world occurs in repeated cycles of payback for the most recent outrage from our enemies, which in turn was justified by them as a response to our own attacks, and so on and so on. With a moment's reflection, it is clear that a great deal of the world's violence could be prevented if people could stop these cycles. But we are acccustomed to these cycles, because the pattern is repetitive. We tell ourselves that this is normal, natural, the way things have always been. Some even object to nonviolence as abnormal and unnatural, perhaps because they are so unfamiliar with it.

Fifth, although violence and hostility are real threats to everyone, we do not often teach the ideas and methods of nonviolence. We could teach them if we chose to do so; the knowledge is available. However, to propose that nonviolence be taught in schools is very controversial in many communities. In some places the objection is that it is not an academic subject. In others nonviolence is greeted with the suspicion that it is religion, or that it is politically slanted. Other communities will claim that they do not need it, even as bullying goes on in school hallways and among students on the internet, teenage drivers (in imitation of their elders) succumb to road rage, and badly handled emotions lead to partner abuse, battering, and rape.

This list of obstacles could be extended, but already it provides a glimpse of what could be called resistance to nonviolence: a complex of barriers and paradoxical elements in human life, which prevent us from taking greater advantage of nonviolence to live more successfully. The good news is that when we come to understand these barriers, their power lessens, and we can then overcome and move beyond them.

Welcomed Nonetheless

Resistance to nonviolence is based on some real fears and concerns, which teachers of nonviolence should acknowledge. When people's feelings of vulnerability and need for security are respected, the rich and inclusive version of nonviolence that we are talking about here will be welcomed by most audiences.

Nonviolence is perhaps most warmly welcomed in communities where violence is overt and prevalent. Although people may carry the old stereotype of nonviolence with them when they come in for a workshop or presentation, and although their initial response may be slightly cynical or suspicious, audiences usually recognize quickly that "this nonviolence stuff" is important knowledge to have. A teacher often senses that there is a widespread hunger for the ideas and skills of nonviolence, a hunger which most schools and other institutions apparently do little to satisfy.

Is Nonviolence Applicable to All Levels of Conflict?

As a working hypothesis, we will claim that the basic ideas of nonviolence are applicable all the way from the individual and interpersonal levels of human life and problem solving, up to the societal and global levels.

These levels have certain features in common. For one thing, every intentional act of violence, from the individual to the international, seems to possess a compelling rationale in the mind of at least one human being. Here are some examples: One man was only trying to "teach my wife a lesson" when he beat her up. Another said he had no choice, because the other guy at the bar had given him "the look." A young woman felt justified in slapping her child because the kid just wouldn't shut up, even after she had yelled at him. A general ordered his troops to destroy a village in retaliation for a sniper attack, and called in air support to eliminate an enemy gun position. In a talk on just-war theory, a national security advisor attempted to summarize the conditions under which it is rational and proper to wage war. This advisor had given similar speeches about three recent wars, finding in each case that the conditions for a just war had been satisfied.

Are there similar brain pathways involved in the experience of felt necessity and justification in all of these cases? We suspect the answer is yes. Cognition and emotion are quite important for understanding what is going on before, during, and after violence.[4] If we learn that a person committed an act of violence, we can be fairly sure that the person perceived (correctly or mistakenly) that he or she had been threatened, disrespected, or harmed by somebody else. Or they may have been afraid that they were about to lose power and control over someone like a spouse or partner, or a vital resource such as oil. There was almost certainly a personal logic, in the mind of the violent actor, that rationalized his or her violence. James Gilligan has argued that almost all violent actors have previously experienced intense shame, or personal disrespect, and so believe that they are acting out of justifiable self-defense, self-protection, or self-assertion.[5]

Another aspect of violence that seems to run the gamut of levels, from personal conflicts to wars, is a tendency by the agents of violence to discount the "collateral damage" caused by their behavior. Violence causes both intentional effects (harm done that the violent actor meant to cause) and incidental effects (harm done that was not intended). Collateral damage is a euphemism for the incidental, unintended destruction of violence, but the labels "collateral" and "incidental" are cruelly meaningless to the people who are harmed. Effects are effects. There is no law of nature saying that the intended effects of violence will be the only significant ones, the most lasting, the most remembered, or the only ones for which the initiators of the violence will be held responsible. In fact, damage that one party regards as "collateral" may very well become the reason in another's mind for the next round of retaliation.

The subjectivity and arbitrariness of what is called collateral damage are greatly under-appreciated by violent people. The main thing on a typical violent person's mind, at the time of the violence, is a highly personal fantasy about control, revenge, punishment, destruction, or "winning." The imagined consequences of the violence make up a distorted cartoon, in which the enemy is eliminated or neutralized, and the problem of the moment is therefore solved. It never turns out to be as surgically effective in real life as it was in the violent person's mind; there are always messy collateral consequences, every bit as real as any intentional damage that was inflicted. But at the time of the violence, these downstream consequences are conveniently minimized in the mind of the violent actor. One of the factors that undermines the credibility of "just war" claims is that the cost-benefit calculations that ostensibly precede a decision to wage war, are inevitably rigged by this discounting of the costs of collateral damage.[6]

We claim that nonviolence has important things to teach us about these and other problems, which range from individual problem-solving to the global level. We do acknowledge that the difficulties in applying nonviolence are significant and daunting. However, one advantage of adopting a broadly inclusive vision of nonviolence is that the full range of human creativity and potential for constructive problem-solving can then be brought to bear.

How Much Nonviolence Do We Need to Learn?

Even a small dose of nonviolence education can affect a person's thinking about conflict and the options available for dealing with it. Chapter 2 contains several reaction papers written by students who had simply viewed two short documentaries about the use of nonviolence, one a story from India about Gandhi, and the other an episode about the sit-ins that were part of the American Civil Rights Movement. The two stories combined took less than an hour to watch, and they are available online if you would like to reenact what the students did. However, just reading Chapter 2 will give you a fascinating glimpse into the range of constructive thought sparked by these two examples of nonviolence.

Systematic training is a higher dose of education than watching videos, and yields more profound effects. But what does nonviolence training involve? Chapter 3 outlines a version of nonviolence training in the King tradition, explaining what is covered in a typical two-day workshop, and how. We think the logic of the training will make sense to you, but that you will nevertheless encounter some surprises. For one thing, the range of topics covered in the workshop may be wider than you thought it would be.

Chapter 4 attempts to convey some sense of the expanded view of nonviolence, and of the world and life itself, that many people gain from experiencing such a training and from further study of nonviolence.

Chapter 5 addresses the task of making nonviolence real, in two ways. First, research that has evaluated the effectiveness of nonviolence is briefly reviewed; and second, the application of nonviolence in police work and the military is described.

We have developed and delivered nonviolence education programs for people of all ages, from many backgrounds and in many walks of life. Therefore the language used here is deliberately secular, although it can be adapted to the needs of almost any group. The companion volume, *Agape and Ahimsa: Twin Roots of Nonviolence*, complements this book by discussing the historical origins of nonviolence in Christianity and in Hinduism, and may be especially appropriate for use in religious settings.

If you are new to nonviolence, we hope these books will open up the topic for you, and leave you eager to learn more. If you are already familiar with one or more of the traditions of nonviolence, we hope that our presentation of these ideas will provide a valuable new slant on this fascinating, vitally important, and inherently interdisciplinary and multicultural field of study.

Chapter 2 - What Students Learned From Two Nonviolent Movements

Although nonviolence is not a traditional school subject, and although most students in the United States receive almost no instruction in it, it is remarkable that even a brief exposure to nonviolence elicits strong feelings, and quick recognition that it is important.

The student reaction papers in this chapter were written by students in a General Psychology class at the University of Rhode Island's College of Continuing Education in Providence. The students were diverse in age, racial and ethnic identification, and gender. The course introduced Psychology by presenting five general perspectives on the field, of which one was termed the Sociocultural.[7] Within the Sociocultural part of the course, topics such as prejudice and stereotypes, power and social influence, cultural identity, and group processes were discussed.

One morning, the class viewed two segments from the Public Broadcasting series on nonviolence movements, *A Force More Powerful*.[8] The first documentary focused on the 1960 Nashville sit-in movement, in which our colleague and friend Bernard LaFayette Jr. had been one of the student leaders. The second documentary was about the 1930 Salt March led by

Mohandas Gandhi in India. Students were asked to write a short reaction paper on what they had seen.

The scope of each documentary will be described next, and then the students will take over with their reactions.

The Two Movements

Nashville, 1960

There are many nonviolent movements from around the world that are now available for study.[9] The one chosen by the producers of *A Force More Powerful* to represent the U.S. civil rights struggle was the Nashville sit-in and boycott campaign of 1960. The sit-ins in Greenville North Carolina, Nashville Tennessee, and subsequently in many other communities, stand as an intermediate phase between the early events of the Civil Rights Movement such as the Montgomery bus boycott, and the later campaigns such as Birmingham and Selma, which changed federal laws. It has been argued that the Nashville campaign convinced Martin Luther King Jr. to place renewed emphasis on nonviolent direct action, and so set the stage for the campaigns of the mid-1960s that produced the Civil Rights Act of 1964 and the Voting Rights Act of 1965. David Halberstam has recounted the story of the Nashville movement and its impact in some detail, in his book *The Children*.[10]

In the winter of 1959-60, Diane Nash, Bernard LaFayette Jr., John Lewis, James Bevel, and other students at Nashville colleges began to attend evening workshops on nonviolence let by Rev. James Lawson. Martin Luther King Jr. had asked Lawson to come south from Ohio to teach Gandhian methods to young people interested in challenging the Jim Crow system of racial segregation. In the workshops, Lawson's young friends learned about the term *ahimsa*, and Lawson connected it to the Christian ideal of love, *agape*. They discussed the successes of nonviolent campaigns under Gandhi's leadership in India, and earlier in South Africa. They debated how to respond to threats and intimidation nonviolently, without impulsively provoking an escalation of violence. They practiced sitting quietly in rows while their friends role-played white bigots who taunted and even physically attacked them.

The students organized a strategy for desegregating lunch counters in several downtown department stores, by having groups of black and white students sit down together and order food. They were refused service as a matter of store policy, because the stores at that time could discriminate against black customers. The white reaction to the sit-ins progressed during the first weeks of the campaign from amazed inaction to semi-organized resistance. Groups of young white men attacked the students, as had been anticipated in the workshops. The demonstrators, following their training, did not retaliate. However, they were arrested and jailed, while their attackers were not charged - a contrast that was soon noted. The nonviolent strategy increasingly drew national attention to the cause of desegregation, and stimulated open questioning of Nashville's official stance on what was legally allowed in the city and what was not.

After a bomb blast destroyed the house of Z. Alexander Looby, the students' legal counsel, there was a march to City Hall, which received a high level of media attention. Diane Nash confronted Ben West, the mayor of Nashville, with the question whether it was right for stores to discriminate against some of their customers on the basis of their color. With the cameras running, the mayor declared that it was not right. This dramatic declaration was the beginning of a process that desegregated Nashville's businesses and other public facilities once and for all.

This successful nonviolence campaign deserves to be more widely known. The video segment from A Force More Powerful is a very good introduction to this piece of American history.

After viewing the Nashville documentary, the students watched another half-hour video about Mohandas K. Gandhi, the person whose work earlier in the 20th century had inspired Lawson and provided a model for the Nashville demonstrations.

India, 1930

Gandhi's two careers were long and rather complicated. He became known as a proponent and leader of nonviolent social change during his first career as an attorney in South Africa. After returning to his native India in 1915, his second career was devoted to moving India toward independence from British colonial rule. *A Force More Powerful* provides succinct glimpses into the two careers. The introduction to the series begins in a South African jail, and notes not only Gandhi's contribution to the early struggles for human rights in that country, but also his influence on many nonviolent movements of the 20th Century which were to follow. The documentary we watched focused on the Salt March, providing a visually compelling illustration of Gandhi's methods and an overview of the struggle for Indian independence.

In March of 1930 Gandhi, by now a revered nonviolent "saint" throughout much of India, chose the British tax on salt as the target of a direct action campaign. Britain enforced a monopoly on the manufacture of salt in India, and imposed a sales tax on it. Salt was a relatively minor part of the overall economy of the British Raj, but the impact of the salt tax was felt by everyone, and especially the very poor. Furthermore, as a symbol of unreasonable exploitation, the salt tax could be understood to represent a much wider array of grievances. The campaign was initiated by marching 240 miles from Ahmedabad to Dandi, on the seacoast, where salt would be made for free in defiance of the British law.

In several ways, the Salt March exemplified Gandhi's approach to noncooperation with unjust systems. It focused on a specific issue, the salt tax, rather than everything at once. It entailed discipline and planning; his core group of marchers were members of his own ashram, who understood nonviolence and the purpose of the demonstration. It was extended over a period of time to allow attention to be drawn to the issue; at about 10 miles per day, it took many days to walk 240 miles. It provided opportunities for many people to participate in very simple ways; a supporter of the march could participate by illegally evaporating sea water to recover the salt.

As the documentary makes clear, the Salt March and other actions of the campaign against the salt tax did not immediately produce a dramatic change in India's status. But they set the stage for later political developments leading to independence, and they provided mythic stories that helped Indians to know their own power and to appreciate nonviolence as an instrument of change.

India and Pakistan have had a turbulent history since their independence in 1947 from the old British Raj, and their partition at that time into two countries (now three; the nation of Bangladesh is the former East Pakistan.) However, a feeling of pride in the cultural legacy of Gandhi's nonviolence remains strong; the prevailing view is that Gandhi now belongs to the world, but his home, and the origins of his thinking, remain India.

The Reaction Papers

These short student papers are reactions, not to a full course or workshop on nonviolence, but to less than an hour of exposure to stories that emphasize nonviolent approaches to social change. The views of the students sometimes support the points we have made about nonviolence in other chapters of this book, and sometimes advance contrary ideas or associate the documentaries with other stories and concepts that were meaningful to the individual writers. The reaction papers, from 12 of the 30 students in the class, were selected for their conceptual diversity and for how clearly the writer's ideas were expressed. We particularly invite readers of this book who are teachers to reflect on this sampling of initial thoughts on nonviolence. We have done only minor editing (principally spelling corrections) of the students' writing; we felt that the flavor and meaning of the original papers came through best if we let them speak for themselves as much as possible. However, we did add the subtitles.

The students' stories are intrinsically compelling, but may be even more so if the reader takes an hour to see what the students saw in class. We recommend viewing the two documentaries from the series *A Force More Powerful*. The title of the Nashville story is *We Were Warriors*. The title of the Salt March story is simply *India*.

Disbelief

My reaction to these two films is very easy for me to write about. First, I cannot believe that I did not learn about this in high school. I feel like this is an injustice to me. When I left class last Wednesday, I felt like I wanted to know more about these two movements in history. These movements give such an important message to people. Dedication and teamwork can make anything happen!

The Jim Lawson workshops were awesome. The message was so clear that a nonviolent approach actually meant fighting back. Fighting with nonviolence may seem like more of a challenge, but it is the way people are won over. The way they sat-in every Saturday in the diners, even though they were being beaten over it is such an inspiration. They knew that their arrests dramatized their grievances in a positive way, so it was worth every bit of agony for them. They had to deal with a mayor who claimed to uphold the law but supported the store owners (and men who broke the law by assaulting the students). They were addressing the country and the world with these acts. The progress they made, although it took about three years, was astonishing. Their perseverance is so uplifting. It is good knowing that if something in this world needs to be done, we can do it. We just need to stick together and make people aware.

I was so interested in Mahatma Gandhi. He really was a saint. His way of communicating to the people how and why they were going to be free was very clever. How did he even know that if they made their own salt and clothes, the British would be less powerful? And most importantly, how would one guy get 350 million Indians free from the powerful British government? Because Gandhi was a nonviolent warrior, he won over many people. The government did lose control, because of violence. When police became brutal to Indians, the British civilians began not following the government so strongly. Their violence backfired on them. Although Gandhi was arrested and was eventually assassinated, his work was not in vain. Everything cannot change at once, but Gandhi definitely made something huge happen.

- R. C.

Anger

Viewing the film on non-violent demonstrations and peace, my main reaction is anger. I feel as if the Southern blacks did not have a choice. If they had reacted violently the results would have most likely been death, or jail. Blacks were not given the opportunity to express themselves, the laws were designed against them, and they did not have many advocates. To resort to violence would have probably increased the odds against them.

I am trying to understand the thoughts and actions of the Southern white people. The people seemed unaware of the degradation and horror that must have surrounded these people at this time. To put in place laws that did not allow human beings to utilize even the basic necessities like a bathroom, to me is just not rational. To deny children equal education and opportunity is sinful. The action of these people is a clear contradiction of their professed Christianity.

The idea of non-violence appeals to me in this instance, only because it worked. The Southern blacks achieved what they set out to achieve, but I imagine myself in the same situation and the anger is overwhelming. I feel the whites should have been beaten and segregated and denied certain rights. I would like to see what the outcome would have been. I do not believe white people would have resorted to a nonviolent protest. I do not believe that they would have the staying power that the blacks demonstrated.

I believe it took intelligence and will for the blacks to carry out an act of non-violence, but my anger is not allowing me to see the psychology in what they did. I cannot speak for all people of color, but if I were to guess, I would say that the majority would have reacted to non-violence with violence.

- C. R.

The Sympathy of Bystanders

The movie we watched in class was very interesting. The students in Nashville used the same method of nonviolence that Gandhi used to bring attention and change to the society they lived in. The approach of nonviolence was very effective. When Gandhi used this approach to get rid of British rule it made the officers look real evil and mean hearted. The reason is looking at footage of police officers beating people in the street looks terrible because the people are not fighting back. It makes a person wonder "How can somebody beat a man or woman for no reason and the person they are beating is not fighting back?" It makes an observer want to listen to the side of the person who is getting beaten because it makes the other side look like savages. That is why Gandhi received a lot of press from all over, even in America. The same goes for people in the South.

This approach of nonviolence worked when the people in Nashville and the people in India were organized, had a leader, and were consistent. I'm sure if people were not organized with a leader the Indian people wouldn't have gotten their freedom and African Americans would not have gotten the equality they wanted in the South. If only some people followed the nonviolence approach and others did not, things would not have changed in the British Empire or America because if the people who felt they were being oppressed fought back with fists and guns they would have looked like rebels and it would have made the things they were fighting for really nonexistent. The nonviolence approach is a weapon that affects the way a person or people see a situation and when people in Nashville and all across America saw what was going on it brought about change in the South, and the same goes for India.

Another thing I thought about while watching the movie was the nonviolence approach does not just involve the two oppositions but has a third part which is the observer or observers. An example of this is a real life one. I used to go to Classical High School, and I used to go to Kennedy Plaza to wait for buses with my friends sometimes and there used to be a lot of fights there. One time there was a fight where it was approximately four on five. And the kids were going at it, each one throwing wild punches at each other with yelling and screaming. After the fight was broken up you could hear some people saying things like "Well, there kids go again fighting downtown," and "I swear kids love fighting in Kennedy Plaza!" Another time I was downtown there was another fight in which two kids got jumped by three kids. The three kids who jumped them were swinging at the two kids hard, but the only thing the two kids did was cover themselves for protection against the blows until the fight was stopped. They did not throw one punch and even after the fight they did not yell in anger, just looked in disbelief. After the fight some people actually went up to the kids to see if they were all right. Now if you compare these two different instances you can see how the nonviolence approach affects people. In the first case, all of the kids were fighting and the people watching were looking at it like "oh well, there's fighting again." In the second case where the two kids who were getting jumped did not fight back, some people came to them to see if they were all right. So in conclusion somehow the nonviolence approach affects people watching the situation, bringing out their compassion and concern about what is going on.

    - P. H.

Closer and Closer to Home

Last week in class we watched a movie titled "A Force More Powerful." This film was about nonviolence and how people today and in the past have changed the world through nonviolence. The term nonviolence is defined as the fight to win someone over without using violence. This film held a very powerful message that I think everyone has to think about and apply it in his or her life.

The first historical event using nonviolence was in Nashville, Tennessee, in 1960. A group was formed to try to desegregate the town's lunchrooms and have everyone dine together. They set out on a Saturday morning by having blacks sit at the diner counters for hours trying to get served. The groups were eventually arrested but had other groups fill in for them directly afterwards. This sent the town into an uproar, no one was injured right away, and eventually it worked. I thought that during this time in history a challenge like this was very courageous. Though the challenge used nonviolence, the lawyer representing the black students had his house bombed. It seems like no matter what technique is used violence is always present in some form or another. Though it is awful to say, sometimes it may seem like the only way.

The true inspiration for nonviolence in America was Gandhi, who set out on a nonviolent task thirty years prior to the sit-ins in Tennessee. Gandhi walked to the beaches of India, setting out to make his own salt and not pay tax, emphasizing injustice to the poor. Though these types of historic leaders are practicing civil disobedience, they are not physically harming people to get their point across. Today it seems no one thinks in these terms. I am personally a large supporter of nonviolence and feel anything can get solved by using this technique. Though I can honestly say I experience violence almost day to day. Whether it is seeing a parent scold a child the wrong way, disrespecting peers or witnessing a fight at a bar, it is all around us. I really thought this film showed a positive message that everyone should learn about in large cities and rural areas.

I come from a small town in Western Massachusetts and in high school there were two groups that were always fighting with each other. I'm sure that if they talked it out they would realize they have a lot in common and that words can get distorted and lead to violence. I thought this video offered a lot of positive information and it really made me think about my personal experiences.

- E. T.

Unthinking Ways

In the movies that we watched in class the one on Gandhi really opened my eyes about what we as a people need to do to overcome all our fears of other races and religions. If there was a force out there that could make all of the races on earth come together and force them to talk about their differences, this would show all of the people that we can all get along together without violence. This would also show people that everybody has the same fears about others, and finally break down the barrier of ignorance. The movies also showed me that the best way to beat an unfair system is to do it nonviolently. This way they cannot make excuses for beating people up or throwing them in jail. The movie showed me that most people don't even think for themselves, they just do what people tell them to do because they don't know how to think on their own. They didn't stop and think that African Americans are people too who have feelings. When Diane Nash asked the mayor if it was fair how African Americans were being treated, he had to stop and think about that question, and finally he said it was not fair. This is an example of how people don't think about the consequences of their actions because they never had to. The South was run like that for years, and after a few generations it becomes a system that everybody follows blindly.

One of the strong points in the movie was when Gandhi started to walk to the ocean and make salt illegally. He picked up a lot of people on the way that felt the same way he did about their oppressors. They felt this way because they were being taxed on something that they needed; they couldn't get around paying for salt because the Viceroy made all the laws and would have them thrown in jail. This is another example of people not caring for another group of people; the Viceroy didn't think of the Indian people as equals, but as second-class citizens or less. If someone had made the Viceroy think about what he was doing or questioned whether the British were there in India for any good reason, it would have made a lot of difference. Perhaps he would have opened his eyes and questioned the point of treating people unfairly. This brings up the point I stated earlier about most people don't even think for themselves. Stanley Milgram's experiment on obedience is related to this.[11]

- A. S.

Bravery and Gratitude

I did not know that Gandhi invented the nonviolence protest tactic. Gandhi's idea was a remarkable beginning to a new era of freedom, not only for his country of India, but for other countries around the world. His protest walk to the salt beach seemed like a small accomplishment at first, but as news of Gandhi's march got around to other communities, more and more people joined his walk for freedom against Great Britain. Regardless of the serious consequences Great Britain placed upon Gandhi and his followers, they continued on with the protest. Gandhi's cause was for the freedom of the Indian people. By believing in this cause, Gandhi knew that he might die because of it. For Gandhi, this was all worth it. Forty years later Americans did the same thing. Black Americans were tired and upset with the segregation between blacks and whites in their community. The African Americans started the civil rights movement against segregated businesses, schools, and jobs in their communities. I agree 100% with this cause and respect every person who was involved with the civil rights movement.

I thank all of these brave heroes for my freedom that I have today.

The death and abuse that the African American men, women, and children experienced was so sad. To think that people can be so cruel to humans because of their race! Today, America has come a long way from the 1960s, but America still needs repair work when it comes to fairness between races. Dr. Martin Luther King Jr., Gandhi, and other civil rights leaders and protesters, served a great purpose for the freedom that we have in the world today. We as the new generation must continue the nonviolent fight for rights and peace for all races around the world.

- J. R.

Perspective

After seeing the two documentaries last week, a lot of things were put into perspective for me. I had no idea how bad things seemed to get back then and what lengths were gone through to make things change. I completely congratulate every single person involved in the "lunch room sit-ins." What a great idea to make known that no one was going to stop them from getting the respect that was very obviously deserved. Those students who did that must have had some outrageous courage to do just a little of what they did. They had to know that they had the chance of getting beat, hurt, and even possibly killed just to get their points across to everyone else.

Being white, I am ashamed of all the white people who attacked those black students just for sitting at their "all white counters." Who were they to decide who could and could not sit there? They were not and never would be God, so that was never up to them. Just the fact that those students were arrested for sitting at a counter was horrible in my eyes. What did they do wrong? All they were doing was fighting for the rights that they, as humans, deserved and were not getting. Gandhi was obviously a great inspiration to those students as well as to all of the other millions of people who go along with the "nonviolence" idea. I personally think that this should be enforced all the time. Just looking at what happened here proves that though it may take time, it is possible to win battles by using brains over force and brutality. Is that a hard concept to grasp or what? Obviously, it must be, because though things have changed a lot, things will never be the way they should be. Every single person in this country, in the world, should have the rights they deserve. Being in the U.S. means a person has rights and shall be treated as an equal. Nowhere in that sentence does it say except for color. We need to enforce that, and not be so mean to people just because they aren't white. Color means nothing, brains mean everything. I really like what Gandhi stood for and believe what he fought for and taught his followers were right.

- A. P.

The World Is One

Conflict is everywhere. Sixteen year olds are blowing themselves up in the name of God. Countries threaten each other with trade embargoes and increasing oil costs. Everyone wants it her/his way or no way at all and if anyone disagrees they will be conquered or destroyed. We disrespect our environment; we disrespect each other; and we disrespect that which is greater than ourselves. The world has forgotten that it is one and it must be shared. It has forgotten that boundaries and borders are defined because the human race has deemed it so.

The film on nonviolence presented in class last week showed us how influential leaders of the past avoided violence while fueling major social movements. People such as Mohandas Gandhi and Martin Luther King Jr. were not willing to accept the injustices of the world and expressed their discontent through nonviolent action. I believe many people are equally discontented with society in the 21st century as Gandhi and King were in the 20th. Yet we continuously overlook the importance of nonviolent action. People are showing their anger through fighting and nothing is changing except the increasing amount of violence in the world.

Furthermore, we have become so consumed with individual gain that it has created a great deal of isolationism; for it is much easier to stay in one's own little world than to see the world of one's fellow human being. We must cease inconsiderateness and gradually begin to decrease the level of ignorance we have of one another's lifestyles. A small adjustment in an individual's life, such as using public transportation or walking as often as possible, is a nonviolent action that leads to a decrease in oil consumption which then leads to decreasing the power of oil moguls; a slight decrease but a decrease nonetheless.

Nonviolent action is crucial to making us realize that the world is one and it must be shared as equally as humanly possible. Humanity can decrease violent conflict. We just need to show that we care through what we buy, eat, and drive. The world will shift slowly but effectively. Our choices must clarify that we reject violence and no longer fear peace.

- J. P.

Worth Fighting For

To begin with, I have to say that this video on nonviolence truly inspired me. There are not too many people these days that will stand up for what is right in order to make a change. Rather, every day you hear the world complain about what should be done in order to create justice and equality. Personally, I feel that it takes courage and strength to stand up for what you believe in nonviolently.

While watching the movie I gained a lot of insight about what it's like to be mistreated and underprivileged, but I had never really thought about the strength and power it took to overcome these tribulations. Every day of my life I experience other people's mistreatment and even sometimes my own, and it is the worst feeling in the world to not be able to change it and feel overpowered. However, I no longer complain. I have learned now that action does speak louder than words, so instead I gather my thoughts and spread knowledge among those that are intimidated by authority. The African Americans in Nashville fought for their freedom and American status. They encouraged me to believe that all things are worth fighting for, even the small things. In further thought, the nonsense that goes on at my job allows me to step one foot in the door. For example, a majority of my co-workers feel threatened by the management staff, who abuse their authority to the max. Therefore, I took it upon myself to write a letter to the district manager of the company. But it does not stop there; I am now held accountable to speak on behalf of the staff at the next store meeting.

In conclusion, I now know that the struggle may be long and may unfortunately have no result, but it is worth the defeat. Nobody in this world should have to live their life without dignity, but sadly to say, it happens. More people should realize that life is worth fighting for no matter what the circumstances. However, what we must remember is that you kill evil with kindness, nonviolently. Nothing in this world will ever be equal, but with inspiring people like Gandhi and Diane Nash, the power, strength, and courage is all mine.

- L. O.

Respect

I hold the utmost degree of respect for the Fisk University students, their supporters concerning the events in Nashville, as well as for Gandhi, his supporters, and their persistent efforts to bring about change through nonviolence. This is truly remarkable, because I feel so few are capable of achieving change by this method. That is, pursuing change in defiance of the status quo and the oppression that accompanies it. It takes quite a unique individual, and furthermore an individual who is part of something much larger, who is one soul joined with the souls of many others in unison to further the movement.

When most people think of nonviolence movements the name Martin Luther King Jr. virtually always comes to mind first, and the 1960s peace marches and sit-ins join those first thoughts. For most, Gandhi's movements are overshadowed by those of the 1960s, yet essentially it all began with Gandhi 30 years earlier and one could say that his policies served as a model for those who were soon to begin in our country. I admire him because he was the first to demonstrate that sacrifices would have to be made for the ultimate betterment of the majority.

In the (psychology) textbook this is defined as altruism. I do not observe too many practicing this today. The decrease of morally sound individuals and the increase of greedy individuals are in part what our society has come to today. Some may argue that perhaps we see less altruism today because there is less in terms of legal injustices to protest, but I disagree. I feel there is much to be done and I remember it every time I drive down the street and see a police vehicle. Unfortunately, I do not feel that we will ever approach this kind of greatness again. The world is much more violent than it has ever been, and that is reflected in people's refusal to cooperate with one another and in their actions towards one another.

For the type of movement we saw in Nashville in 1960 and for the greater part of the decade was systematic. There was concern that if one or two people lost their nerve and submitted to violence, it would have jeopardized the whole thing. It was mentioned in the documentary that this is what their opposition wanted to see happen. They saw it as a passing fad, and thought it would soon go away with arrests, beatings, and other forms of intimidation. Instead it has gone down in history as something much more, because of the exercise of moral discipline and teamwork.

- M. M.

Taught Me A Lot

In the PBS special we watched two segments both dealing with nonviolent protest. The first segment dealt with segregation in Tennessee and the second segment was about Gandhi. Both segments taught me a lot about nonviolence.

In the first episode, we watched the segregation in Tennessee. The episode taught all about nonviolent demonstration. The demonstrators used different means other than violence to get their message across to the white members of the community. The black demonstrators first tried to desegregate counters in restaurants. The way they did this was by using three groups of people that came in, one group after the other groups were arrested. The second episode was about Gandhi and how he marched members of his movement to the sea. While watching Gandhi I did not really agree with him, because all he did was march and collect different members throughout the communities. I did agree with how he asked different members of the government to step down from their positions. I did agree with this because it breaks down the chain of command.

Before I watched this movie the only kind of demonstrations I was used to was the violent type. I have watched on television the L.A. riots as well as many other ones. I never realized that it could be done in a nonviolent way. By watching these segments it showed me that more is accomplished from nonviolence than violence. Not as many people die, and people get their message across more effectively by not hurting anyone. This really shows me that they stand for what they believe in.

- J. H.

What is "Normal"?

While watching these videos in class, I can feel myself wishing it were more like this everywhere. It can be hard for some to relate to this nonviolent method of bringing changes to the world. I would guess this goes back as far as when we were children. The *Tough Guise* issue would also apply here.[12] If we were not taught to fight with weapons and violence, if it were not "normal," how different things might be in the world. I once told my husband that if we were involved in a war, I would take my grandson far away so he would never have to kill another person or be killed himself. My husband was very upset by this and I really do understand why. He went into the Army right out of high school and made a career of it. He truly believes a man should fight for his country and protect his family. I too believe this, yet I pray for a different answer or a different method. People do what they feel to be normal or what they are taught to be right. He was raised to think this way like many men. How do we change this type of thinking?

In watching, I came to the conclusion that it took more bravery for those people to stand tough with no violence or weapons than it took for any of the officials with their clubs and guns at their sides. People who use force as a means to settle something are not using their God-given gift of thought. I realize these men are being given orders to use force, but this does not make it all right. Here is an example of Milgram's obedience study where we follow orders no matter who we hurt. We can also see Zimbardo's study is evident in how things can get carried away when a little power is involved.[13] Fear is also a big factor in how we react to a situation. We may be more forceful if we are more frightened.

People who use force and follow orders are only doing what is natural in this day and age. It is what we see all around us in every aspect of our life. If we started with our children in schools and showed them other ways to solve issues and ways of nonviolence, we may have a chance to change our current beliefs. Maybe if we showed both sides of an issue and how we have dealt with it in the past, children would see the nonviolent way as a better method. It is very hard to look at both sides of an issue when only one side is visible. I do not recall ever seeing one thing about nonviolent methods in all my years in school. This is the first time I have actually become aware of it. I had heard of Martin Luther King, Jr. And Gandhi but never really knew what they represented. Hopefully in our future years our children and their children will find a more peaceful way to communicate and discuss matters of the world.

- E. H.

Thoughts on the Reaction Papers

There are some themes in the students' writing that teachers of nonviolence will probably recognize. First, the students saw the relevance of nonviolence to core human concerns. There is eloquence in the way many of them expressed their feelings about these core concerns. There is an acknowledged lack of past education and information about nonviolence. There is amazement and disbelief that such important material would be withheld from children and from people generally. There are emotions such as anger evoked by the oppression against which nonviolence has often stood. There are insights derived, such as the idea that what seems normal to us is determined by what we have been taught. There are corrections of belief, such as learning that not all "demonstrations" are violent. Important questions get raised, such as whether great leadership is necessary for nonviolence to be effective. Finally, there are fascinating individual variations in what people notice and emphasize, in how they feel, and in the conclusions they draw.

Nonviolence elicits strong feelings and significant, sometimes uncomfortable, thoughts about education and about life in general. It is a topic that stirs almost everyone to some degree, upon even brief exposure. Furthermore, most people find that they want to identify with the goals of nonviolence and to express their admiration for its struggles and accomplishments. It is remarkable that a subject not widely known or heard about can so quickly command sympathetic understanding, expressed in so many different ways.

Chapter 3 - What Goes On in a Nonviolence Training?

"Training" usually means a period of supervised practice in a skill or discipline, undertaken to achieve a higher degree of proficiency. We can see athletic, musical, vocational, and military training, among others, as fitting this definition of the term. Deliberately nonviolent thinking and acting are relatively unfamiliar, at least as skills, to most of us. Going through the experience of nonviolence training is an excellent way to become more familiar with nonviolence quickly.

Short-term nonviolence training has played an important role in preparing demonstrators and other workers in social change movements all over the world for what they would encounter as they set out to improve conditions in their communities. For some, whether they have been active in a social change movement or not, the initial experience of nonviolence training is also the beginning of a lifelong educational process leading to higher levels of mastery of this "third way" of thinking about life.[14]

"So, what do you actually do in one of these nonviolence trainings?" We get this question a lot. What follows is not a complete answer, because some of nonviolence training involves experiential and cooperative learning; that is, being right there in a training session or workshop with other people is much more powerful than reading about it. But there is no big mystery to nonviolence training, and here we will try to give a sense of how a workshop is put together and some of the content conveyed to the participants.

We will describe a workshop in Kingian Nonviolence, which is based on the work and writing of Martin Luther King, Jr. There are several other excellent approaches to nonviolence (for example, those of the American Friends Service Committee and the Fellowship of Reconciliation), and we regard the one described here as belonging to a family of related trainings. Some training approaches are Gandhian, some emphasize a religious tradition, some stress social change, and so on. Therefore, while the many varieties of nonviolence training and education do overlap, they are also complementary to each other. One approach will pay more attention to some aspects of nonviolence than others do, and together the different approaches make up a large mosaic of ideas and areas of application.

The Kingian approach described here was developed primarily by Dr. Bernard LaFayette, Jr., in collaboration with his colleagues David C. Jehnsen and Charles Alphin, Sr. Dr. LaFayette was an an active participant in the Civil Rights Movement, and worked closely with Dr. King.[15] In Dr.LaFayette's approach, an intensive two-day training experience is the preferred vehicle for introducing nonviolence while doing justice to King's ideas. Here is a typical sequence of topics for a two-day "core" workshop. This list will also serve as an outline of this chapter:

Topics in Kingian Nonviolence Training

Introduction of Participants
Finding Positive Common Ground
Analyzing Conflict: Types, Levels, and
Distances
Adversarial and Hegelian Understandings of
Conflict
Historical Perspective: Five Successful
Nonviolent Campaigns
King's Principles of Nonviolence
Steps for Nonviolent Problem-Solving
Using Top-Down and Bottom-Up Planning
Large-Scale Group Exercise
Closing

Trainers are often asked to present shorter workshops, and the content would then be abbreviated. However, even in a shortened training or presentation we would include some historical perspective on Martin Luther King's work, the Principles of Nonviolence, and the Steps for Nonviolent Problem Solving.

Using the full list of topics, let us go through the two-day training plan, and consider each component in turn.

Introduction of Participants

The initial introduction of group members to one another is treated, not as preliminary to the training, but as one of its integral stages. Introductions are done in such a way that individuals begin to learn about each other as people, get on their feet and talk, and get a taste of standing in someone else's shoes. Our usual procedure is to have each group member talk with another person for about five minutes, and share answers to some specific questions such as "Where did you grow up?," "What is one thing that most people would never suspect about you?," and "Where would you go on your ideal vacation?" After this period of conversation, we ask each person to introduce their partner to the entire group, with a first-person twist: each person assumes the name and identity of their partner. So if Sally and Ron had been paired for the initial conversation, Sally would start her introduction by saying, "Hi, I'm Ron ... ," and then go on to relate what she has just learned about Ron, but in the first person.

After all the introductions have been made, the trainers can debrief by asking two kinds of questions. First are questions about what it was like to pretend to be someone else: Was this awkward? Why? Were you nervous about the correctness of the information you were giving? And so on. Second are questions about what it was like to be introduced by someone else: Did they "get" you? Were you appreciative that they listened to you so well? And so on. Each group of individuals will come up with its own insights about this exercise.

This type of introduction is a good ice-breaker both for groups of strangers and for groups of co-workers or students who are already acquainted with each other. Taking time for the conversations makes the process of getting started less rushed and more personal. Also, assuming the identity of another person gives a preview of "putting yourself in another's shoes," which is a meaningful skill for practicing nonviolence.

Finding Positive Common Ground

People have many positive qualities. They admire good qualities in others, such as strength, humor, quick-wittedness, compassion, and the ability to overcome adversity. They value their important relationships with friends and mentors, recognize the value of learning, and - across many religions and cultures - they understand that a reverence for life, the world, and others is a good thing. We often use an exercise early in the training workshop to establish that each person in the group has good values, that others do too, and that therefore there is reason to identify with other people and respect them and ourselves for being similar in good ways. There are several specific exercises that can help accomplish these goals. Our favorite is one we will call S/Heroes, a term meant to include both heroes (male) and sheroes (female).

We ask participants to think back over their own lives, and focus on people who have had a strong positive influence on them. To generate more s/heroes, we ask them to think of at least one important person from the first half of their life so far, and one from the second half. We also ask participants in the workshop to name the contribution each s/hero made to their lives, or the value the s/hero represents to them. Then we invite people to share who they have been thinking of, and why those s/heroes have been important to them.

One person might recall that his mother taught him how to make it through hard times. Another might say that her high school volleyball coach was the person who showed her that working hard produced results. Another might credit an older child at school as being the model for how to stay calm in a conflict. As each person contributes, we build lists of the s/heroes and values. Typically, as each person speaks, several others in the group will be seen nodding their heads in understanding. It is not unusual for a few tears to be shed as members of the group tell these mini-stories about their own lives.

Each person will speak from deep conviction, because these are stories from their own experience, and are key pieces of their own personal history. The nods and expressions of emotion from others in the group are an indication that this trading of stories touches something in each of us that could be called common ground - a "better side of human nature" that is not owned exclusively by some, but is almost universally shared by people everywhere.

Our better side needs to be supported, and one goal of nonviolence training is to provide that kind of support. Now, it is true that people have negative qualities too. Every day we receive many reminders that other people can mislead us or be dangerous to us. Our suspicions of others receive support from news stories about shootings and fights, road rage and domestic violence, corruption and brutality. Sometimes this negative bombardment makes it seem that there are two kinds of people, the good and the bad. But in fact, each of us contains both some of the good and some of the bad. In Martin Luther King's words, every one of us has the potential for both great good and great evil. The Russian novelist Alexander Solzhenitsyn expressed the idea this way:

"Gradually it was disclosed to me that the line separating good and evil passes not through states, not between classes, nor between political parties either - but right through every human heart, and through all human hearts." [16]

We advise the members of our training group that the good side of an enemy, and therefore a large part of our potential commonality with him or her, is very easy to forget. The person that we dislike today almost certainly admires many of the same qualities that we do, and shares many positive qualities with us. But anger and hatred create a strong tendency to dehumanize our opponents. We forget that they are people like us. We also forget that they, or others like them, will still be there tomorrow, and we will again need to interact with them.

Remembering the humanity of our opponents, especially when we are angry, is another skill in the practice of nonviolence. Like other skills, it can be improved through practice. During training, we start the practice in a calm and friendly atmosphere. Most of us will benefit from further practice, however; the times when this skill is most needed are also the times when it will be most difficult.

Analyzing Conflict: Types, Levels, and Distances

Conflict is an inescapable part of life. Differences of perspective, experience, vested interest, ambition, and preference lead us to disagree with each other and to compete with each other. Sometimes human beings seem to crave conflict; we even invent new conflicts in the form of games, sports, and debates. Conflict can teach, invigorate, and entertain. However, we all know that conflict can also get out of hand. Arguments can escalate into violence. In order to understand the origins of violence, and our options for responding to it, it is helpful to take an analytical look at different types and levels of conflict, and at different distances from a conflict where a person may be located.

Types of Conflict

Let's look at four types of conflict, termed pathway, mutually exclusive, distributive, and value.

In a **pathway conflict**, the people who are in conflict actually have the same goal, but disagree over how to achieve it. For example, two friends may want to go to Cleveland to visit the Rock and Roll Hall of Fame. But one person wants to go as quickly as possible on the interstate highway, and the other wants to take a more scenic and leisurely route. Their conflict is not over where to go, but how to get there. **Mutually exclusive conflict** (also called goal conflict) involves people who disagree about their goals, but who must continue to function together because of family, work, or other ties. We ask our group to generate examples of pathway and goal conflicts in the family, at work, and in the community. **Distributive conflict** describes a situation in which there are not enough resources, and people are fighting for their share. A family example would be two teenagers both wanting to use their mother's car. **Value conflict** involves a fundamental disagreement over beliefs regarding right and wrong. The conflicts over abortion rights, gender equality, gun control, and capital punishment, are familiar examples.

Distinguishing different types of conflict can help us to discern what people still have in common (but are likely to forget or minimize), despite their current differences over paths, goals, resources, or values. For example, people in a pathway conflict have a common goal. People in a goal conflict are "stuck together" in the same family or workplace. People fighting over resources have their need for those resources in common. And people in a values conflict, as we have seen, share many positive human qualities that tend to be forgotten in the heat of battle.

It should be said that the types of conflict described here are not sharply and objectively different. To some extent viewing a conflict as one type rather than other is a choice. Most conflicts have a value dimension, especially to the participants. The important training outcome at this stage is acquiring the view that conflicts can be analyzed, and that the structure of the conflict may contain helpful clues for a participant, or an interested bystander, to move toward a solution.

Levels of Conflict

Second, it is useful to examine three levels of conflict that may affect a person's options for practicing nonviolence: normal, pervasive, and overt.

Normal conflict means disagreement or competition that is carried on within accepted rules. Participants want to win the conflict, but do not hate or despise their opponent. If people can be said to crave conflict, it must also be said that

most of the time, it is normal conflict that they most desire –
playing sports or games, debating with friends, and so on.
Pervasive or heated conflict occurs when tempers rise. The
rules that govern normal conflict are tested and bent as
emotions flood the participants' bodies, their voices get louder,
their body language becomes combative or defensive, and their
thoughts and words begin to dehumanize the opponent, setting
that person up as a target to be attacked rather than a person
deserving respect and consideration. **Overt** conflict involves
actual fighting.

When does "violence" start? For many people, the third
level, overt conflict, would be the very definition of violence.
However, from the perspective of nonviolence, it is at the
second level, pervasive or emotionally heated conflict, that
violence emerges and the need to control it begins. Kingian
Nonviolence does not define normal conflict as a form of
violence. Thus, it is possible, and even desirable, to have
normal pathway, goal, distributive, and value conflicts - all
without violence.

The goal of nonviolence is not to eliminate conflict. In
fact, sometimes the goal is to create it. As practitioners of
nonviolence, we are interested in maintaining constructive
effort at the normal level of conflict, preventing escalation to
the other levels, and intervening to de-escalate to the normal
level when necessary. In order to do this, we must develop
skills for managing conflict.

In a workshop, we may point toward this need for learning skills using role-playing exercises on identifying types and levels of conflict. One or two pairs of participants act out a conflict, and others observe and try to classify the type and level that is being portrayed. Based on this analysis, we then discuss approaches for managing or solving the conflict.

Distance from a Conflict

A third dimension of conflict is a person's distance from it. You may be in the very middle of it as a **participant**, or nearby watching it unfold as a **bystander**, or you may be farther away as a **remote observer**. For each of these distances, there would be a range of nonviolent options. Importantly, this range of options widens as distance from the conflict increases. This means that a participant in conflict may have very few options, a bystander more options, and a remote observer many. Now, although the remote observer has the most opportunity to change the conditions and even the social structures that lead to conflict, he or she may also have little motivation to do so. Motivation, meaning the urgency with which a person seeks to solve the conflict, diminishes with distance, being greatest for participants, less for bystanders, and least for remote observers.

Let us briefly consider the options available to bystanders, who are often in the best position to intervene in conflicts constructively. William Ury, an authority on negotiation, has listed ten roles that a "third side" can play in a conflict. Three of these roles pertain to prevention, and so are relevant early in the development of a conflict: the provider, the teacher, and the bridge-builder. Four of the roles pertain to resolving ongoing conflict: the mediator, the arbiter, the equalizer, and the healer. Finally, three of the roles address the containment of conflict: the witness, the referee, and the peacekeeper. For more on these roles, we recommend Ury's book, *Getting to Peace*.[17]

Adversarial and Hegelian Understandings of Conflict

Most of us perceive conflict in terms of two adversaries opposed to each other. We assume that the conflict is a contest between these two sides, and that one side will win and the other lose. Martin Luther King was influenced by the philosopher G.W.F. Hegel to view conflict in another way. Consider this quote from one of Dr. King's sermons:

"But life at its best is a creative synthesis of opposites in fruitful harmony. The philosopher Hegel said that truth is found neither in the thesis nor the antithesis, but in an emergent synthesis which reconciles the two." [18]

The terms thesis, antithesis, and synthesis are from Hegel's treatment of how conflicts evolve over time. The perspective offered by Hegel is that conflicts have a past and a future; the contest we see before us in the present is part of a larger whole. Today's contest between two adversaries is like a still picture taken out of a movie. Unlike artificial conflicts such as a baseball game, the two sides in a real everyday conflict may both win, or they may both lose. They may not even stay the same people throughout the conflict, because of changes in their knowledge or interests. Conditions may also change because of the intervention of other people. When a new synthesis, a third position acceptable to both of the adversaries, is found, both sides win.

Dr. King saw opportunity in this way of viewing conflict. He suggested that creative, nonviolent leadership could often shape the progress of conflicts toward reconciliation of the original adversaries.

How can we discover a synthesis that can reconcile the conflicting positions of thesis and antithesis? There is no formula that will guarantee a satisfactory result. However, there is an approach that is worth trying, and we introduce it in training as a way of turning the Hegelian view of conflict into a rational procedure. In this approach, we look for "threads of truth" - that is, valid points or legitimate needs and interests - in both thesis and antithesis. Combining the threads of truth from the two opposed positions can give us a "first draft" of a synthesis. At the very least, this exercise gives a third way to look at the overall problem.

Dr. King used this approach to derive an understanding

of nonviolence itself. Many times, people are faced with a threat or offense, and feel they must decide between fighting back or just letting it go without responding; they experience an internal conflict, in which the thesis is violence, and the antithesis is passivity. Now, what is a truth, or a good quality, about violence? Well, violence is at least active; it involves doing something in response to an injustice. What is a truth, or a good quality, about passivity? Well, passivity is unlikely to hurt people through direct retaliation against the aggressor or the collateral damage that would follow it. Nonviolence, in Dr. King's derivation, combines the activity of violence with the non-injury of passivity; it is an active response to injustice that seeks no harm. In this way, Dr. King was able to explain nonviolence to his followers, and to clear up for them the mistaken notion that nonviolence means passively letting injustice happen. Furthermore, from their knowledge of Dr. King's accomplishments, his listeners could see that most of those achievements fit this definition.

Historical Perspective

The most active period of the Civil Rights Movement was 1955-1968, the years during which Dr. King and others led campaigns to end legal segregation of the races in the southern United States. A nonviolence workshop cannot teach all of this history, but we do sketch the stories of five campaigns that illustrate the successful use of nonviolence training in community change: the Montgomery bus boycott, the Nashville sit-ins, the Freedom Rides, the Birmingham civil rights campaign, and the Selma voting rights campaign. For each campaign, we aim to review the issue that was addressed, identify some of the people involved, describe the methods used, and be clear about the result that was achieved. We encourage our participants to study the history of nonviolence in greater detail; for many, this becomes an enduring avocation.

Montgomery, 1955-56

In Montgomery, Alabama in 1955, the city bus system was segregated under local law, and was notorious in the city's black community for daily mistreatment and humiliation of non-white riders. On December 1, 1955, Rosa Parks was arrested for refusing to give up her seat on a city bus to a white person. Martin Luther King, Jr., a recently-arrived pastor, was chosen to head the Montgomery Improvement Association, which organized a boycott of the city buses that lasted for 381 days. The boycott was opposed by leaders of the white community, and by white supremacists who bombed Dr. King's home. Dr. King insisted on nonviolence throughout the boycott, and won national attention and support for the cause of desegregation. A Supreme Court decision late in 1956 declared the segregated bus system unconstitutional, ending the boycott.

Nashville, 1960

The famous tactic of "sitting in" at segregated lunch counters did not start first in Nashville; sit-ins had been used sporadically at least since the 1930s as an attempt to change race-based discrimination. However, in February 1960 the famous Greensboro NC sit-ins at Woolworths set off a wave of sit-ins across the United States. Nashville's sit-ins were led by a remarkable group of young college and seminary students, including Diane Nash, John Lewis, and Bernard LaFayette Jr., who had been studying nonviolence under Jim Lawson, and preparing for a challenge to segregation in their city. Peaceful sit-ins at several downtown lunch counters were followed by a general boycott that drastically affected business during the pre-Easter shopping season. After the racially motivated bombing of the home of Z. Alexander Looby, the students' legal counsel, there was a march of several thousand protesters to City Hall, where Diane Nash confronted the mayor, Ben West, and asked him directly whether he could personally defend segregation. He declared that he could not, and from that point on, the desegregation of central Nashville made progress. The students from the Nashville group went on to play major roles in other campaigns of the Civil Rights Movement - some, including Bernard LaFayette, serving on Dr. King's staff.

Freedom Rides, 1961

The Freedom Rides were undertaken in 1961 to

challenge southern states to enforce federal laws desegregating interstate bus facilities such as washrooms and waiting rooms in bus stations. James Farmer, head of the Congress of Racial Equality (CORE), decided to draw attention to the still-segregated facilities by having a mixed group of black and white people ride Greyhound and Trailways buses from Washington DC to New Orleans. The Freedom Riders were violently attacked in Alabama at Anniston, again in Birmingham, and again in Montgomery. Trained in nonviolence, they did not retaliate in kind. Additional riders, beginning with trained student leaders from Nashville, joined the Rides. They were determined that violence would not succeed against the effort to desegregate interstate transportation. As a result of the Freedom Rides, Attorney General Robert Kennedy instructed the Interstate Commerce Commission to actually enforce the law, and desegregate the busing facilities. Signs for separate "Whites Only" and "Colored" facilities began to disappear.

Birmingham, 1963

In 1963, one hundred years after President Lincoln's Emancipation Proclamation officially ended most slavery, Birmingham, Alabama was, according to Dr. King, the most segregated city in America. The downtown business district allowed black citizens to spend money, but not to sit at lunch counters or to use the stores' fitting rooms or washrooms. Martin Luther King Jr., Fred Shuttlesworth, and others led a boycott of the downtown businesses seeking to desegregate stores and increase their hiring of black employees. There were marches and demonstrations, resulting in the arrests of many people, including Dr. King. It was during this campaign that he wrote the famous Letter From Birmingham Jail. Marches across Kelly Ingram Park by young demonstrators were met by police violence in the form of dogs and fire hoses ordered by the commissioner of public safety, Eugene "Bull" Connor. This greatly embarrassed President Kennedy's administration in its international efforts to promote American values. An agreement was eventually negotiated between Dr. King and the city, which served as a preview of the federal Civil Rights Act of 1964.

Selma, 1965

The voting rights of black people in the south were severely restricted, and this further diminished their ability to serve on juries and run for public office. Thus, gaining and exercising the right to vote constituted a critical step in the push for greater racial justice. The campaign in Selma, Alabama in 1965 was part of a major effort by the Southern Christian Leadership Conference, the Student Nonviolent Coordinating Committee, and other groups, to increase the number of black citizens who were registered to vote. Martin Luther King, John Lewis, Hosea Williams, Ralph Abernathy, and other leaders organized three attempts to march from Selma to Montgomery, the state capitol. On Bloody Sunday, March 7, the marchers were beaten by police and a mounted posse as they crossed the Edmund Pettus Bridge. Television broadcasts showing nonviolent demonstrators being ridden down and beaten shocked millions of viewers. The final march to Montgomery took place two weeks later with participants from across the nation, including many clergy (author Ira Zepp was one) who returned home and preached about voting rights and citizenship. The Selma campaign led directly to passage of the federal Voting Rights Act of 1965, which made barriers to voter registration and voting illegal.

A Note on Martyrs of the Movement

Three people died during the Selma campaign. The first was Jimmy Lee Jackson, 26, a deacon in his Baptist church, who was shot by a police officer after a peaceful demonstration in Marion, Alabama during the early days of the campaign. The second was Rev. James Reeb, 38, who was attacked by segregationists the evening following Dr. King's second march to the Edmund Pettus Bridge, which had ended with prayer and a return to Selma in observance of a court injunction. The third was Viola Liuzzo, 39, a housewife and civil rights activist from Detroit who had come to Selma as a volunteer to help with the voting rights campaign by serving as a driver. After the completion of the third march, she was shot and killed by the Ku Klux Klan while driving with another civil rights worker, Leroy Moton. Moton survived by pretending to be dead.

Rev. Reeb and Viola Liuzzo were both members of the Unitarian Universalist denomination. Ever since the Selma campaign, the UU church has taken a special interest in civil rights history, and especially the cause of voting rights for which Jimmy Lee Jackson, James Reeb, and Viola Liuzzo gave their lives.

Challenging a society that is willing to violently resist you in your work for justice can obviously be frightening. These deaths reinforce the fears of many people that standing up for a cause nonviolently is a dangerous thing to do - and indeed it is.

However, during the 14-year period from 1954 to 1968, relatively few people died in the U.S. struggle for civil rights, at least when compared to the much larger number of deaths in leaderless riots at home or in the wars of that time abroad. Just forty names appear on sculptor Maya Lin's Civil Rights Memorial at the Southern Poverty Law Center in Montgomery, Alabama. A book published by the Center tells the stories of these 40 martyrs.[19]

Principles of Nonviolence

The heart of this Kingian nonviolence training can be found in the chapter called "Pilgrimage to Nonviolence," in Martin Luther King's first book, Stride Toward Freedom.[20] Dr. King pauses in the middle of his book about the Montgomery bus boycott to explain the development of his approach to nonviolence. He reviews his educational history and some of the intellectual influences he carried away from his studies at Morehouse College, Crozer Theological Seminary, and Boston University.[21] Dr. King positions himself in critical opposition to both capitalism and communism, although he finds valuable ideals in both. He distinguishes nonviolence from pacifism. And then, in the last few pages of the chapter, he presents six principles of nonviolence that, for him, are the guiding principles of the boycott and of his overall mission. In nonviolence training we present these principles, and get our groups to alternately challenge and defend them.

Martin Luther King's Six Principles of Nonviolence

King's Principles speak both to the nature of nonviolence and to some of our most deeply rooted fears. They also address some serious misunderstandings that many people have about how their lives intersect with those of others. Here is the list of principles; alternative wordings, including Dr. King's own phrases, are given that express the main ideas for different audiences.

1. **Nonviolence is a way of life for courageous people.** In Dr. King's words, "… nonviolence is not a method for cowards." For young people: Nonviolence takes courage.

2. **The Beloved Community is the framework for the future.** In Dr. King's words, "… (nonviolence) does not

seek to defeat or humiliate the opponent, but to win his friendship and understanding." For young people: Turn enemies into friends.

3. **Attack the forces of evil, but not the people who are doing evil.** In Dr. King's words: "... the attack is directed against the forces of evil rather than against persons ..." For young people: Focus on the problem, not on "problem people."

4. **Accept suffering without retaliation for the sake of the cause.** In Dr. King's words: "... a willingness to accept suffering without retaliation, to accept blows from the opponent without striking back." For young people: Every good thing has a cost. For police and military trainees: Sacrifice may be necessary.

5. **Avoid internal violence of the spirit as well as external physical violence.** In Dr. King's words: "... (nonviolence) avoids not only external physical violence but also internal violence of the spirit. ... At the center of nonviolence stands the principle of love." For young people: Cultivate love to replace hatred.

6. **The universe is on the side of justice.** In Dr. King's words: "... (nonviolence) is based on the conviction that the universe is on the side of justice. Consequently, the believer in nonviolence has deep faith in the future." For young people, and for volunteers who risk burnout: Justice is possible, so keep

at it.

Sample Objections to Each of King's Principles

King's six principles challenge human beings to take a moral "high road." While they are obviously nice ideas, and social pressure may lead some to pay lip service to them, the principles are not taken seriously by many people under normal circumstances – at least, not at first. Occasionally, through hard experience or through sudden insight, people are won over on their own to the view of life that the principles exemplify.

Waiting for sudden insight is not a recommended teaching strategy, however. Another path is to spend some time during nonviolence training on both the reasons for adopting these ideals and the practical difficulties of living up to them. Interestingly, upon hearing the principles, most people inwardly recognize that they want to accept them, but fear that the real world makes it too difficult to do so. Here are some typical "but" reactions to each principle:

1. Nonviolence Takes Courage

But: "Nonviolence means not wanting to fight. Sounds like being a coward to me."

2. The Beloved Community

But: "Community? Why should I put up with people I

don't like?"

3. **Attacking Evil, not People**.

But: "What about evil people? Don't they deserve to be attacked?"

4. **Suffering may be Necessary**.

But: "Isn't it stupid to let yourself - a good person - get hurt?"

5. **Internal Violence and Love**.

But: "My feelings are what they are, violent or not. It's healthy to let them out."

6. **A Just Universe**.

But: "Are you kidding? The world is going to hell in a handbasket."

These common objections reveal some strong initial resistance to nonviolence. Note that several of the objections reveal feelings of distrust and fear. Remarkably, we often defend ourselves against nonviolence as if it were a threat to us! One of the reasons Martin Luther King stood out as a great leader is that he challenged this resistance. He suggested that the reasons for nonviolence are so strong that we need to overcome our fears of it. How would Dr. King answer the objections listed above, and others like them?

That question can be turned into a training exercise. Let us consider each objection in turn, and how Dr. King, or someone thinking very much like him, would respond to it.

Imagining Dr. King Responding to Each Objection

In a training workshop, participants would spend time in small groups generating challenging questions about King's Principles, similar to those we have just imagined. Then, working on the questions posed by others, each group would try to formulate some answers to the questions, answers that Dr. King himself might have given. This practice in "thinking like King" avoids pressuring people into a premature uncritical acceptance of nonviolence, and provides insight into nonviolence as a way of thinking that can be learned.

To illustrate some possible products of this exercise, here are some responses to the objections that were given to each principle, written while imagining how Martin Luther King's voice might have sounded in expressing a nonviolent perspective.

Objection to Principle 1, which is about courage: **Nonviolence means not wanting to fight. Sounds like being a coward to me**.

Response: *Courage is often tied up in the desire to be a man, and so the first principle is primarily directed to those who have this desire. But young boys, full of bravado and physical courage, are often* *frightened by the prospect of embarrassment and ridicule. Once a mean-spirited bullying mood sets in among their friends, they are compelled by this fear to go along. Is this courage? No. It is conformity to peer pressure.*

(Now, it must be said that peer pressure is just as strong for most adults as it is for these young boys. But we often talk unfairly about the young as if peer pressure were exclusively their problem.)

The courage referred to in the first principle is often not physical courage, but the courage to act rightly rather than in conformity with group pressure.

On the other hand, the readiness to fight is often not a sign of courage, but a giving-in to impulse, panic, and expectations.

Nonviolence asks us to measure our responses to others, and not to be confused about what requires courage.

Objection to Principle 2, which is about the "beloved community": **Community? Why should I put up with people I don't like?**

Response: *The second principle provides a test that we can all use to determine whether we are moving toward this ideal called the beloved community, or away from it. The test is this: Are we seeking to defeat and humiliate our opponent? Or are we trying to win his friendship and understanding? If the first answer is "No," and the second answer is "Yes," then we are heading in the right direction.*

That is, how we act toward our enemies is the test of whether we are moving toward or away from the world envisioned by nonviolence.

It is admittedly difficult to look beyond the moment and decide to treat our enemy decently. But that is precisely what nonviolence challenges us to do.

In the thoughtful words of Abraham Lincoln, "Am I not destroying my enemies when I make friends of them?"

Objection to Principle 3, which is about attacking problems, not people: **What about evil people? Don't they deserve to be attacked?**

Response: *The third principle asks us to keep "personalities" out of our efforts to solve problems. Here we must remember that people are not simply good or bad, but a complex mixture of traits and tendencies. Although human beings have a tendency to demonize their enemies, this tendency does little to resolve conflicts, and often escalates them unnecessarily.*

We are often diverted from solving problems because we fix our emotional energy on revenge against individuals, and because upon getting our revenge by hurting or incarcerating the guilty, we just stop.

Studies of violent criminals support the idea that even very "bad" men are a tragic mixture of beliefs, defenses, and vulnerabilities which invite sympathy upon close examination, and which hold clues to rehabilitation.[22] The terrible damage done by some of these inmates is evidence not just of personal depravity but of external conditions that, if changed, could have averted the damage. Their stories are instructive about how we could prevent violence by changing the conditions out of which it grows.

Why should we stop attacking persons, when that feels like such a natural thing to do? We should stop because that kind of attack sets up a continuing cycle of hostile retaliation, and does nothing to bring greater justice or to solve the problems in which both we and our opponents are enmeshed.[23]

Objection to Principle 4, which is about suffering: **Isn't it stupid to let yourself - a good person - get hurt?**

Response: *We must acknowledge that many people seem to experience a great fear of nonviolence, because they suspect that a commitment to nonviolence may call for suffering. This suffering may occur when a nonviolent person is attacked by a violent person. More commonly, it may occur whenever a nonviolent person stands up and puts him- or herself in an uncomfortable position for a good cause.*

However, it should be emphasized that the fourth principle does not send people out to endure suffering for its own sake. There is already plenty of suffering in the world, some of it accidental and some of it intentional. Most of this suffering, especially the intentional kind, is unnecessary.

The suffering at issue is the purposeful suffering, or sacrifice, that may be necessary to right a wrong, and which therefore can be redemptive, not only for the person who suffers, but for others as well.

In our real world, the choice to be nonviolent may lead to suffering for the sake of a just cause. But the choice to be violent always leads to suffering, usually to no good purpose.

Objection to Principle 5, which is about replacing violent feelings with love: **My feelings are what they are, violent or not. It's healthy to let them out.**

Response: *It is true that human beings are susceptible to strong feelings of resentment and hostility. Many people believe reflexively that these feelings constitute a force of nature that cannot, and even should not, be controlled.*

But we are not entirely helpless in the face of these emotions. We have the power to cultivate the kind of love called agape as a benevolent emotion to replace internal violence of the spirit. And we have the obligation to do so.

People steer their own emotional lives all the time. We do this by spending time with our family and friends, through meditation and prayer, and with music and reading and reflection.

The violence that we seek to replace with nonviolence originates within the human heart. Our resentments and hatred therefore hurt us first, and most. Fortunately, we have the ability to steer away from this violence within us, by reminding ourselves of the humanity of our enemies, and by engaging in the important work of enlisting their help in the cause of justice.

Objection to Principle 6, which is about progress toward

justice: **Are you kidding? The world is going to hell in a handbasket.**

Response: *For many of us, there is a religious foundation for the belief that the universe is on the side of justice. Therefore, it is perhaps easier for the faithful to be confident about this principle than it is for more secular proponents of nonviolence.*

One secular way to think about this principle is in terms of what world people would prefer to live in. Imagine that the events in the human universe can be sorted into five boxes: the intentionally good, the accidentally good, the neutral, the accidentally bad, and the intentionally bad. When asked to change the universe by throwing out one box, almost everyone chooses to discard the box containing intentionally bad events. This strong preference is evidence that the scales of the universe are tipped toward the good.

Now, the universe may lean toward justice, but that is not enough. The universe is full of tools, but they will be ineffective unless we pick them up and use them. We must pick them up, use them, and keep on using them. And that brings up the value of persistence.

This sixth principle is important because persistence in the face of resistance is important. Frustration, at least for a while, is the inevitable consequence of challenging the status quo. And the duration of this frustration is uncertain. Combating burnout among those who work for justice and human betterment is a constant mental health issue, which leaders of a movement must acknowledge and confront.

But here is the good news. Persistence works. The great examples of social change of the past hundred years or more have happened at tipping points in our history, prepared for by years of quiet work beforehand. We may not be able to predict when these points will come, but we can be confident that working steadily for justice will one day bring the needed change.

Aggression and Conciliation

The Aggression-Conciliation Model is an outgrowth of Dr. King's second and third principles. The second principle is about treating your opponent in a conflict as a potential ally. The third principle is about not personally attacking human beings whose actions may have been evil, but instead attacking the evil in unjust situations.

The Model looks like this:

YOU		PROBLEM
Aggression	==>	Conditions
Conciliation	==>	Persons

Let's say that YOU (on the left side of the diagram) face a PROBLEM (on the right). Broadly speaking, you have two large sets of possible responses to the problem. The first, Aggression, consists of all the high-energy, attacking, oppositional things that you are capable of. The second, Conciliation, consists of all the ways you can be accepting and respectful.

The Problem also has two parts, called Conditions and Persons. Conditions are what some scholars call the "systemic" or "structural" aspects of the Problem, which exist regardless of the people who are involved. Persons are the individuals who play roles that enforce or benefit from those conditions, the actors that you confront at the present moment.

The diagram of the Aggression-Conciliation Model shows a guide for how to direct your responses appropriately with the aim of solving the Problem. Two conscious choices are recommended: directing your Aggression toward the Conditions (which echoes King's third principle), and directing your Conciliation toward Persons (which echoes King's second principle).

The model also recommends that two errors be avoided: directing Aggression toward Persons, which tends to set up a cycle of hostility and violence, and directing Conciliation toward Conditions, which amounts to accepting the Problem without trying to solve it.

Participants in a workshop can be asked to analyze a community or family conflict and make recommendations for how it might be handled differently, using the Aggression-Conciliation Model as a guide. Some examples: People in a poor neighborhood might resent the owner of a convenience store, the only place within walking distance where they can buy food. Or: A mother has daily fights with her daughter over the loud music she plays after school. Or: Freshman college roommates are in conflict over how to control the traffic of friends who visit their dorm room.

The Aggression-Conciliation Model is appealing because of its symmetry and completeness in comparison to other approaches. We have found that the Model can help to dispel the misconception that nonviolence wants people to completely suppress their anger and aggression. For example, a young man approached one of us after a workshop and thanked the trainers especially for teaching him about aggression and conciliation. He explained that the model did more than just repeat the often-heard demand that he not fight with people. The part about directing Aggression toward Conditions "gives me something to do with my anger," he said.

Finally, it is important to keep in mind that the Persons on the right side of the diagram also have a choice to make about how to use their own capacities for Aggression and Conciliation. In fact, to them, you are really one of the Persons who is part of their "Problem." Both of you possess human strengths and weaknesses that it behooves you both to understand. One is that a Hegelian view of conflict offers more options than an adversarial view. Another is that behavior tends to be reciprocated, so that choosing Aggression or Conciliation increases the likelihood that your opponent will choose likewise. Another is that persistence increases your chances of successfully solving the problem, as suggested by Dr. King's sixth principle.

Now, the Aggression-Conciliation Model is not guaranteed to solve your problems quickly; it is only a framework within which some elements of nonviolent problem solving can be assembled and put to work.

Steps for Nonviolent Problem-Solving

Martin Luther King Jr.'S famous *Letter from Birmingham Jail* is a classic essay on purposeful action. It was written as a response to members of the white clergy who had urged Dr. King and his colleagues to avoid confrontation, and instead wait for the gradual progress of civil rights in Birmingham. Dr. King replied in his *Letter* that the time had come for action, and explained that the actions of the campaign to desegregate Birmingham were not impulsive, but the result of a deliberate planning process.

He listed the four steps of this process as follows: "… collection of the facts to determine whether injustices exist; negotiation; self-purification; and direct action." [24] In the training curriculum used today, nonviolent problem-solving is discussed using a framework of six steps whose roots lie in Dr. King's <u>Letter</u>.

Six Steps for Nonviolent Problem-Solving

- **Information Gathering**, also known as Research

- **Education**, involving both Teaching and Learning

- **Personal Commitment**, requiring Reflection and Resolve

- **Negotiation**, to arrive at a Common Description of the Problem

- **Direct Action**, if necessary, to Restart Negotiations

- **Reconciliation**, in which people establish a better Relationship

These steps are meant to be applicable from the individual and family levels to the community and global levels. They stand in contrast to impulsive, hostile, threat-driven responses to problems. The steps are consistent with many prescriptions for rational problem-solving found in business, psychology, and philosophy.

Information Gathering

The first step in nonviolent problem solving -

Information Gathering – derives from Dr. King's phrase "collection of the facts." Often problems can be solved through Information Gathering alone. However, this step deserves some discussion.

From the calm perspective of a reader at home, or a student sitting in a classroom, it may seem obvious that a person should gather information when presented with a problem or a conflict. But information gathering is seldom what people actually do when confronted with an angry neighbor who has a grievance, or a car that won't start, or being fired from a job, or being threatened by harassing phone calls. Our first reaction to being faced with an emotionally charged challenge is often some kind of emotional outburst rather than rational information seeking.

Our first impression of the problem – that is, the first idea we have about what we are facing - is often distorted. After all, we are under stress. Perhaps we have been surprised and knocked out of our familiar routine by the appearance of this new threat. The tendency to seek someone to blame kicks in. Our tendency to interpret conflicts as adversarial kicks in. Our physiology prepares us for fight or flight, and oversimplifies our thinking.

What advice might help a person to step back and start gathering information instead of reacting impulsively to the problem?

A short version of the advice we give is: "Doubt your first impression." The step of information gathering should start with a reminder of this simple suggestion. Training can build the habit of being skeptical about the truth of one's immediate perception of the situation at the beginning of almost any problem. That can open a path to more complete information gathering.

Why is this advice good?

Some of our thinking is fast - it is impressionistic and based on many ingrained assumptions and biases. Fast thinking can quickly reach decisions and guide action. Sometimes fast thinking saves our lives, but more often it leads us into trouble. There is another kind of thinking that is slower, more logical and investigative, and that gives up speed in order to achieve greater accuracy. Our first step of Information Gathering requires us to activate that second, slower, kind of thought. [25]

The need to actively seek out better information can be illustrated by examples generated by the training group. Ask, "Have you ever felt foolish because you jumped right into a conflict, making a totally wrong assumption about what was going on?" Most groups will have no trouble coming up with stories from their own experience, or second-hand stories from friends or from the news. These examples may reveal a variety of insights. Sometimes the information needed to solve a problem is "gathered" by accident, as when I discover the watch that I had thought stolen in the pocket of a pair of jeans I haven't worn for three weeks. Sometimes we change our impressions by learning about the perspective, needs, or motives of another person, as when the bus rider I had criticized for not giving up his seat to an elderly person finally gets up at his stop, retrieves his walker, and slowly leaves the bus using the handicap assist elevator. Sometimes the conflict is over data that is readily available but that no one has yet examined, as when a student challenges my long-held belief about the sources of pollution in the Great Lakes by locating an archive of excellent information on the subject that I had never consulted.

Another habit to develop is openness to different sources of information.

Gandhi famously held that in a conflict, each side owns a piece of the truth. That means we must be willing to accept a part of the solution from someone we regard as an opponent or even an enemy. On the scale of everyday arguments among friends or family members, a good way to put Gandhi's idea into action is to say "You have a point" when you've recognized a part of the truth in what they are saying. Said at the right moment, this simple statement has the power to defuse and re-channel the energy being invested in a conflict. It can also contribute to Information Gathering by you, and by the others in the situation.

Education

As information is being gathered, occasions will arise when the natural next step is to share that information with others. This is Education, an unstated but implicit part of Dr. King's "collection of the facts."

Every problem has stakeholders, people who are affected by the problem and have an interest (a stake) in solving it. The stakeholders are the audience. Information should be given to them that is verifiable, and that will help them contribute to the eventual solution.

It is important to be honest and open about Education. Education is not propaganda. It is not persuasion. It is not lying. Education should be the communication of good relevant information to those who need it, and who are in a position to use it.

At the same time, the message may need to be translated into the language of different groups of stakeholders, and framed to address their interests and ways of thinking. For example, the motivation for renovating a city's playgrounds may be most effectively strengthened among law enforcement officials by emphasizing public safety issues. But the approach to family service agencies might emphasize the benefits to children. The approach to city hall might emphasize the cost of various alternative plans. The same overall problem will look a little different to each of these stakeholder groups.

One is reminded of the fable of the elephant, in which different blind men each experienced the elephant in turn as a wall (because one felt the elephant's side), a tree (because one felt the elephant's leg), and a snake (because one felt the elephant's trunk). The perspectives of different observers will lead to different perceptions of the same reality.

The step of Education should be taken thoughtfully, and should include not only sending information out, but being open to suggestions from stakeholders that may come back in - a continuation of Information Gathering. In fact, these steps are never strictly sequential, but flow back and forth as the problem and its solution unfold.

It is interesting to reflect that Information Gathering is what scholars call "research," and Education is what most people would call "teaching." Research and teaching are the two principle missions of a college or university. When a college is at its best, research and teaching intertwine and inform each other. So should it be in a nonviolent problem solving process.

Personal Commitment

Personal Commitment is the step that Martin Luther King called "self-purification." Dr. King found through experience that difficult problems, once they were well understood, called for courage and strong personal commitment by the people attempting to solve them. For him, serious reflection and a conscious decision to go forward were absolutely necessary.

We have rarely found a step corresponding to Personal Commitment in textbooks on cognitive psychology, or in business school treatments of problem-solving. These disciplines implicitly take the personal commitment of the problem solver as a given. But in the real world, there are times when proceeding with an attempt to solve a problem will be premature and counterproductive. Deciding when and how to move, and whether you are the right person to do it, can determine the success or failure of the process. It is not difficult to see why Martin Luther King considered self-purification a necessary stage in the process of nonviolent problem-solving.

Sometimes the step of Personal Commitment will lead to a decision to go ahead, and sometimes the decision will be to postpone further steps if the problem is not "ripe" to be solved right now, or until additional people are available to join in the task, or other necessary conditions are in effect. In either case, it is important for the decision to be deliberate and based on a good understanding of the situation.

However, the deliberations of Personal Commitment should not be confused with procrastination. Dr. King's Letter from Birmingham Jail is a detailed reflection on the necessity to act. The Letter is a chapter in one of his books, whose very title is *Why We Can't Wait*.[26] The need to pause for a step of Personal

Commitment is coupled with the need to be decisive.

A very important aspect of Personal Commitment is focusing on one tangible and specific goal at a time. During the Nashville sit-ins, there was a moment when Jim Lawson, giving his morning instructions to a group of demonstrators, told them to work in pairs, but to avoid pairing a white person "with a Negro of the opposite sex - because we don't want to fight that battle." At the time, interracial marriage was actually illegal in many states, and even the sight of an interracial couple could ignite opposition to the campaign over an issue not related to the desegregation of lunch counters.[27]

Regrettably, progressive causes often compete with each other for attention, money, time, and people. In a world with so many problems to solve, perhaps this is inevitable. However, in the pursuit of any one goal, it is important to keep the message simple and clear. In part, Personal Commitment is about taking one well-considered step at a time.

Negotiation

The step of Negotiation brings people with different positions together to discuss the problem, to offer proposals, and to more fully understand each other's underlying needs and interests. There are many treatments of negotiation as an art and a set of management skills. Most share the goal of moving the parties who are in conflict closer to a common description of the problem.

Negotiation involves difficult conversations, because the people involved disagree about important issues, and may have personalized the conflict so that they really don't like each other. They may fail to listen to what the other side is saying, and when both sides fall into this trap, little can be accomplished. One skill that helps is Active Listening, in which we consciously stop our own mental rehearsal of what we want to say next, and really listen to the person on the other side of the table. When it is our turn to speak, we first try to restate what we heard the other person saying, in a way that he or she will agree is their position. Only then will we respond to that position with ideas of our own. Active Listening can improve communication between the two sides by demonstrating respect, setting a standard for clarity, revealing competing and common interests, and creating movement toward solving real problems.

One popular approach to Negotiation that has a strong nonviolent flavor is described in the book *Getting to Yes*, by Roger Fisher and colleagues.[28] Like Martin Luther King, the authors of this book recommend close attention to one's opponent in a negotiation, seeking to understand the needs and interests that lie behind that person's public position. Also like Dr. King, *Getting to Yes* stresses the availability of win-win outcomes in most negotiating situations, and emphasizes the desirability of negotiating to a conclusion in which nobody walks away as a loser.

Direct Action

Sometimes, negotiations break down. Here is where the fifth step, Direct Action, may come in. The purpose of Direct Action is to return to the step of Negotiation. In Dr. King's words:

"You may well ask: 'Why direct action? Why sit-ins, marches, and so forth? Isn't negotiation a better path?' You are quite right in calling for negotiation. Indeed, this is the very purpose of direct action. Nonviolent direct action seeks to create such a crisis and foster such a tension that a community which has constantly refused to negotiate is forced to confront the issue."[29]

The "action" chosen should be appropriate to the problem at hand. Sometimes two nonviolent direct actions may take diametrically opposite forms. For example, in the Montgomery boycott people stayed off the city buses, but in the Freedom Rides people rode the interstate buses. Both were forms of Direct Action. In each case, the action was appropriate to the issue, and served to create tension toward changing entrenched segregation.

Note that Direct Action is not the centerpiece of nonviolence, although for many people examples such as sit-ins, boycotts, and marches are the first images that the word nonviolence may bring to mind. Direct Action is the fifth step, not the first. And it is only undertaken conditionally, if earlier steps have not solved the problem. Protests and demonstrations are sometimes carried out impulsively and out of strong emotional reactions to being offended or threatened. However, this type of direct action should be distinguished from actions that are in the spirit of nonviolence.

Some people will point to Dr. King's deliberate fostering of tension through direct action as evidence that he himself used pressure tactics to get what he wanted from his opponents. To these critics, creating tension and crisis does not seem to fit with their idea of nonviolence. In response to this position, we note that nonviolence is an active, not a passive, approach. We also note that in a democracy, using negotiation and nonviolent direct action stand in contrast to bullying by autocrats and bigots, which represents another approach to "problem-solving." Nonviolence achieves results through political rather than violent means, but without guaranteeing that the process will be comfortable for everyone.

Reconciliation

In Dr. King's *Letter From Birmingham Jail*, reconciliation was not mentioned as one of the preparatory steps he had taken before launching the 1963 desegregation campaign in that city. That makes sense, because reconciliation is about the outcome of nonviolent problem solving, not the "front end." At the time the *Letter* was written, Dr. King was still in the middle of the struggle.

Reconciliation represents a high standard for the

outcome of a difficult struggle, especially one in which the parties have begun as enemies. To whatever extent possible, the solution of problems should move the parties closer to the Beloved Community – perhaps much closer, but perhaps only a little closer, for now. Full Reconciliation means that the original opponents in a conflict, and other stakeholders, can respect one another, understand each other's perspectives, and work together constructively.

A friend of ours who is a nonviolence trainer and a police lieutenant keeps the goal of Reconciliation in mind as he deals with perpetrators of crimes and with angry victims. He reports that the thought of Reconciliation tomorrow has a powerful effect on how he interacts with people today who would otherwise "push his buttons."

Often reconciliation is difficult to achieve in the short term. We may have to settle for a disgruntled compromise, or for people "agreeing to disagree," or for parties simply separating so that they do not continue to hurt each other, or for arbitration that leaves one side much less satisfied than the other. In many books, these outcomes count as conflict resolution. We prefer to think of them as temporary solutions that may eventually achieve nonviolent reconciliation. A helpful thought here is that problem-solving does not necessarily follow the timetable in my head, or yours.

Recall that Martin Luther King was influenced by the philosopher Hegel, and particularly by Hegel's dialectical way of viewing conflict. When we encounter a conflict, it appears to be a contest between two positions, the thesis and the antithesis. However, as time passes, these positions may evolve into a new position, the synthesis, which is different from either of the original two sides.

We can think of the step of Reconciliation as a kind of Hegelian synthesis. In the best case, it is a win-win solution to the original conflict, and may not only be a solution but a transformation of that conflict into a quite different situation.

Coordinating Top-Down and Bottom-Up Contributions

Many attempts to solve community problems fail because there is no knowledgeable and respected person on the scene with whom both community members and their political leaders can talk. Authority figures then are prone to make pronouncements that ring hollow to people living in neighborhoods. Average members of the community, who have important things to say, are disregarded by the leaders who have the power to implement their ideas. The people at the grassroots of the problem come to disrespect and caricature the officials in power, and the officials in turn disrespect and belittle the people they are supposed to serve. This kind of dysfunction is found in many communities all over the world.

From a nonviolence perspective, the built-in differences

between official leaders and average community members create a continuing need for bringing "top" and "bottom" together. Nonviolent leadership can seek to bridge the gap between sides that are far apart by fostering more respectful communication. Some of the philosophy and skills of nonviolence introduced earlier in the training can now be applied to this type of situation.

It is very helpful to analyze the conflict using the vocabulary of nonviolence training. We ask our training group to remember that both leaders and ordinary community members are human beings with their own perceptions of the community and its problems. We remember that people may already be making the mistakes of personalizing the conflict (aggression toward persons) or apathetic withdrawal (conciliation toward conditions). We consider that both sides may have some valid points to make (threads of truth in both thesis and antithesis). We hold to the goal of getting people to work together (Principle 2 - seeking not to defeat and humiliate the opponent but to win his or her friendship and understanding). How can nonviolence guide two sides toward a good outcome (Step 6 - reconciliation)?

In general, the nonviolent leader or mediator uses the six steps and the aggression-conciliation approach with each side, repeatedly. With each side in turn, we demonstrate that we understand the problem from that side's point of view, including their needs and aspirations that may extend beyond the current problem. We seek to establish common ground from which the two sides can begin to work together on meeting shared needs.[30] We encourage each side to see the other as a potential ally rather than a permanent enemy. We also encourage each side to consider its relationship to such constituencies in the community as women and minority groups, youth and students, progressive and voluntary organizations, businesses, educational institutions, religious and interfaith settings, and government agencies.

This topic in the Kingian Nonviolence training program has traditionally been called "Top-Down, Bottom-Up." The image is of a nonviolent planner and mediator helping two sides with different roles in the community to create a synthesis out of their originally opposed positions. This role may or may not be successful on our timetable in any specific instance. But it is certain that many community problems have remained unresolved, and many misunderstandings between parts of a community have remained to fester for years, because the community lacked some members who were willing and able to play this role.

Large-Scale Exercise

Throughout a two-day training there are many opportunities for short role-playing exercises, in which group members can act out conflicts, or answer a question as if they were Martin Luther King, for example. Toward the end of the second day, we like to engage the group in a larger-scale exercise that can draw on several skills from the training. Here we describe two exercises, one, The Grid, that is suitable for a group of people that come from different life paths and work experiences, and one, Joy City, that is suitable for a group that already works together and faces real problems that they probably feel they know all too well.

The Grid

Legend has it that Albert Einstein invented a riddle that he thought only 1 or 2% of people would be able to solve. It belongs to a category called grid puzzles, and while they are very difficult for one person to solve alone, they can be somewhat more manageable, and instructive about group interactions, when several people are working on them.

Here is one grid puzzle, Einstein's famous "fish" riddle:

There is a row of five differently colored houses. Each house is occupied by a man with a different nationality. Each man has a different pet, prefers a different drink, and smokes a different brand of cigarettes. There are fifteen clues to aid in solving the riddle:

1. The Scot lives in the Red house.
2. The Swede keeps dogs as pets.
3. The Dane drinks tea.
4. The Green house is next to the White house, on the left.

5. The owner of the Green house drinks coffee.

6. The person who smokes Pall Mall cigarettes rears birds.

7. The owner of the Yellow house smokes Dunhill.

8. The man living in the center house drinks milk.

9. The Norwegian lives in the first house.

10. The man who smokes Blends cigarettes lives next to the one who keeps cats.

11. The man who keeps horses lives next to the man who smokes Dunhill.

12. The man who smokes Blue Master drinks beer.

13. The German smokes Prince.

14. The Norwegian lives next to the Blue house.

15. The man who smokes Blends has a neighbor who drinks water.

Who has fish at home?

Procedure: Print out the 15 clues and the question (i.e. "Who has fish at home?" - the answer to which is the goal of the exercise). Then cut the printed page into strips, each with one of the clues or the question on it. Distribute these slips to the members of the training group, going around repeatedly until all the strips have been given out. Members of the group are instructed not to show their slips to anyone else during the exercise. However, a whiteboard or other display board should be available for organizing information.

Then announce to the group that they have everything they need. Don't answer any further questions.

A typical group will take anywhere from 30 to 60 minutes to solve a puzzle like this one. In the process, they will experience frustrations, and will recognize the need to negotiate over ways to represent the problem visually and incorporate pieces of information. It will be important for the group to ensure that everyone's input is included, because every single clue is needed to solve the puzzle. However, trainers should not give explicit coaching on such points.

Grid puzzles like this are logically solvable, but difficult enough to bring out complex human behavior. They require thoughtful information gathering and, depending on the group dynamics, may require all the other steps of nonviolent problem-solving in order to reach an answer that leaves everyone satisfied.

Joy City

The Joy City exercise can be adapted to the specific circumstances faced by the training group in their workplace or in the community outside the training. It will provide an opportunity for them to delve into familiar problems with the tools developed during the training. Here we sketch a Joy City exercise with hypothetical characteristics and problems to provide a sense of how this part of the training might play out. The details can be adapted to the needs of the actual training group.

Joy City is a medium-sized town of mixed cultures

located about fifty miles from a much larger city in the same part of the U.S. where the group is meeting. There is one high school, grades 9-12, and one junior high school, grades 6-8. In the past few years the calls for police service, drug arrests, and homicides among youth have increased. There have been several fights at the high school since the school year started, and last evening, a young girl was killed by a stray bullet as she left the high school. Witnesses informed the police that a group of youths had been arguing in front of the school with guns just before the shooting started.

The training group is divided into small groups of 3 or 4 people each. The small groups are given 15-20 minutes to do the following:

(1) List information they would need to determine the causes of violence in Joy City.

(2) Indicate how they would involve community leadership and stakeholder groups.

(3) Decide how they would spend a one-time grant of $300,000 (or make actual use of some other significant but limited resource) toward solving the problems faced by the community.

The groups would be asked to work fast, without too much self-censorship, but to draw on the principles, the steps, and other components of the training as they work.

At the end of the small-group work, a trainer would call everyone together for a comparison of ideas. There will be plenty of opinions and a desire for discussion at this stage. Ideas will emerge that range widely in approach, emotional tone, and emphasis. Many proposals will indeed reflect the topics introduced during the training. It is unlikely that one approach will emerge that everyone agrees is the perfect solution. Almost everyone will feel that they have learned something valuable from ideas that others in the group have put forward.

An additional component of Joy City can be a period of Step 1 (information gathering) role playing, in which the small groups visit community officials such as the mayor and the police chief, to learn about their perspectives on the problem. Some individuals would be recruited to play the roles of these officials, and given tips on how to resist requests for information and action, based on such interests as keeping costs under control.

Toward the end of the exercise, most people in the group will be able to recognize ideas that illustrate the philosophy and methods of nonviolence. Where these ideas seem inadequate, group members will often point out how a proposal could be strengthened and still be nonviolent. The idea that **there may not be a perfect solution, but there are nonviolent approaches that are preferable to "enemy-thinking,"** can be voiced by a trainer, but the group will probably see this without the trainer's help.

Closing

At the end of our time with a training group, we like to form a circle and close the training in a way that allows people to reflect briefly on nonviolence and on their experience together. One way to do this is to ask each person to offer one word that captures their reaction to the training and their feelings about nonviolence. Some of the words that we often hear are energizing, humbling, inspiring, transforming, and worthwhile.

Of course, many group members are not able to summarize all their thoughts and feelings in one word. We have often instead heard lengthy dissertations. And that's OK, within reasonable limits.

Based on many training experiences, we have learned that an introduction to nonviolence along the lines we have described in this chapter has several positive effects on most of the members of a training group that they are aware of and appreciate:

- Participants are reminded through the values exercise that each person has good values, and that while there are differences between people, there is also positive common ground to be found.

- The historical perspective part of the training fills in gaps in almost everyone's knowledge of Martin Luther King Jr., about the legacy of the civil rights movement, and about the current concerns and functioning of communities, especially in the United States.

- Addressing conflict as more than just an adversarial head-butting contest, and linking Dr. King's view of conflict to the search for win-win solutions, is often a revelation.

- The training encourages people to examine their own beliefs and values, and to consider discrepancies between values and practices. It challenges people to consider their life choices and the strategies they choose for meeting their needs.

- The affirmation of personal worth and the acceptance of needs, combined with the challenge to change strategies, is almost always seen as an honest approach with real-world implications, that can appeal to at-risk youth and others who are resistant to attempts to change them as people.

- The strength of character and courage required to live nonviolently elevates the approach above the myth that "turning the other cheek" is just a punk's way out, and that anyone who is nonviolent is simply afraid.

- Presented as both philosophy and methodology,

nonviolence "rings true" to many people in management and human service roles. It captures the complexity and texture of everyday work with people by emphasizing the practical value of a positive approach, while not shrinking from the difficulties of dealing with the negative side of human nature.

- Training also allows individuals to begin a potential lifestyle change, not alone, but with a group of people who have shared the training experience. The training is an opportunity for people to make a commitment to a "higher road" with the support of others.

- Many people are surprised to discover that they seem to have been waiting for something like nonviolence to come along. We have been told that the training has energized and given rise to new motivation; that it has transformed how others are viewed; and that it has provided a new framework for thinking about solving problems and managing conflicts.

In conclusion, although we have become strong advocates of this type of training, we try as professional educators and researchers to keep things in perspective. Nonviolence training seems to meet a need, but it must be regarded as a work in progress rather than a finished product. It is a type of intervention that demonstrably has a positive effect on attitudes, knowledge, and skill potential. It also seems adaptable to the needs of many different audiences. As we go forward, we have adopted a "continuous improvement" approach to the further development and evaluation of nonviolence training. We believe that this approach is in keeping with the spirit of nonviolence itself, and with Gandhi's advice to continue experimenting with it.

Chapter 4 - There's More to Nonviolence Than I Thought

"The nonviolent approach does not immediately change the heart of the oppressor. It first does something to the hearts and souls of those committed to it. It gives them new self-respect; it calls up resources of strength and courage that they did not know they had. Finally it reaches the opponent and so stirs his conscience that reconciliation becomes a reality."

Rev. Dr. Martin Luther King, Jr.

On the evening of January 30, 1956 in Montgomery, Alabama, Martin Luther King Jr. stood in front of his home, which had just been bombed.

At the time, he was the leader of the bus boycott, sparked on December 1, 1955 when Rosa Parks refused to give up her seat on a city bus to a white person. The aim of the boycott was to end the city's long-standing official policy of segregating whites and blacks on the city's buses. Facing Dr. King that evening was a crowd of his supporters, angry that their leader's house had been attacked, and especially angry that Mrs. King and the couple's first child, Yolanda, had been placed in danger of losing their lives. Dr. King's friends felt they had plenty of justification to seek revenge. Some of them had brought weapons, and they were ready to retaliate violently against white citizens and their property. All it would take was a word from Martin Luther King.

Dr. King told his friends to go home, and to put away their weapons. He reminded them that their boycott had a great purpose, and that to resort to violence would be to throw all their work away in one instant of madness. He reassured them that he and his family were all right. Somewhat calmed, his followers did as he asked.

In her later recollection of that time, Coretta Scott King picked that night as one of the most important moments of the Civil Rights Movement. The boycott went on to win an important victory in the U.S. Supreme Court, which held that the state and city segregation laws, such as Montgomery's laws requiring segregated buses, were unconstitutional.

Big-Tent Nonviolence

Over the past century, the most famous examples of nonviolence in action have been the campaigns of Mohandas K. Gandhi in India against British colonial rule, and of Martin Luther King, Jr. in the United States to eliminate legalized racial segregation. Nonviolent methods have also been used in opposition to virtually every war of modern times, to the nuclear arms race, to military conscription in many countries, and to many types of economic exploitation and political repression. On another front, the exercise of democratic methods such as voting, and the balance of power among branches of a government can be seen as nonviolent alternatives to violent coercion. So can the rational and humane problem-solving methods of good leaders and managers everywhere. Many of the world's religions and cultures have contributed to the literature of nonviolence. And nonviolence has heroes all over the world, from the Buddha to Baha'u'llah (founder of the Baha'I faith) and from Danilo Dolci ('the Gandhi of Sicily') to Aung San Suu Kyi (recipient of the Nobel Peace Prize for her opposition to the military rulers of Burma). There are many types and flavors of nonviolence all over the world.

The Montgomery bus boycott was the first of Dr. King's major campaigns aimed at ending the American apartheid of legalized racial segregation in the Southern states, and its success made a profound impression all over the world. Importantly, it was a campaign whose success was built on a deliberate commitment to nonviolence.

The story about Dr. King reminding his angry friends of the path they had chosen to walk with him illustrates the understated power of nonviolence as an approach to solving difficult problems. Turning away from violence not only saved lives that night, but also preserved the credibility and momentum of a historic movement for social change. It drew admiration and support for Dr. King and his cause. And it provided an example of people choosing - consciously, strategically - to get beyond their present desire for revenge in order to win a larger prize.

It is easy to recognize an instance of nonviolence when, as in the story about Dr. King on his porch, a person visibly turns away from violence in a historically important conflict where we might have expected violence to break out. But nonviolence is also at work in situations that are less dramatic. Everyday examples of nonviolence also involve turning away from hostility and enemy-thinking:

- In a dispute between family members, nonviolence could mean finding a time to discuss the issue when the anger has mostly subsided.
- In physically threatening situations, nonviolence could mean trying to talk first rather than fighting or giving in.
- In a business negotiation, nonviolence could mean trying to satisfy the other side's needs as well as your own.
- In parenting, nonviolence could mean showing children how to solve problems in a step-by-step way, teaching respect for others, and modeling the values of patience, humor, and responsibility.
- In political action, nonviolence could mean taking the time to understand the positions, motives, interests, needs, capabilities, and limitations of all the parties involved.
- In dealing with highly volatile community conflicts, nonviolence could mean seeking "win-win" solutions in

which everyone's needs and interests are identified and respected.

In all of these situations, nonviolence means working with others respectfully and in a spirit of sensible problem solving. The examples above are stated in positive rather than negative language. They use the word "could" - in part to emphasize that we usually have more than one nonviolent option to choose from. In each example, nonviolence would also include avoiding insults and attempts to degrade or humiliate others, as well as, yes, finally, refraining from physical violence.

Nonviolence is a large topic. It is a rich and rewarding subject for study, practice, reflection, sharing with others, and choosing directions for action. Nonviolence is not one "pure" idea. People with diverse points of view can understand it differently. Some people are nonviolent for strictly practical reasons, because they can only get what they want using nonviolent methods. Other people try to live their whole lives nonviolently, because they believe in nonviolence as a basic principle of ethical living. There are also people who are somewhere in between.

Our view in this book is that nonviolence is a "big tent." Within this tent we find a family of approaches that have much in common, are pulling in roughly the same direction, and include a range of applications from the individual to the global. Nonviolence is not a rigid set of dogmatic rules. It is more inclusive than exclusive, and it welcomes creative discussion of nonviolent approaches to both particular problems and living in general.

Five Aspects of Nonviolence

We propose to break nonviolence down into five parts or aspects: opposition to violence, caring about others, goal-orientation, facing reality, and personal investment. Why are we taking this approach, and why these five aspects?

Over the years, we have introduced nonviolence to many people: students (from elementary school to graduate school), adults in community workshops and churches, and special groups such as prison guards, mental health workers, and teachers. Over and over, people have returned from their first few hours of exploration in nonviolence with such reactions as these:

"There is more to nonviolence than I thought."

"I thought it was just about 'turning the other cheek,' but nonviolence is so much more."

"I had no idea of all the other implications."

"Why didn't I have to take a course on this when I was in school?"

We think that the five aspects of nonviolence discussed here begin to capture what people mean when they say that there is "more to nonviolence" than they had expected. And we have found that almost anyone studying the traditions of nonviolence soon concludes that these aspects are closely intertwined. In keeping with our broad, "big tent" approach, we do not locate nonviolence in any one aspect, but use the term "nonviolence" to tie all of them together.

1. Opposition to Violence

Ahimsa, the Sanskrit term for noninjury, is one of the origins of nonviolence, and is of course at the very core of what people learn from exposure to nonviolence education, whether in training workshops, school or college courses, or through reading.

Being opposed to violence is implied by the very word "nonviolence." What may not be obvious at first is that opposition to violence itself breaks down into more than one idea. There are at least three types of opposition to violence that deserve to be highlighted: (i) not committing violence ourselves (which comes closest to the root idea of *ahimsa*); (ii) not cooperating with violence and oppression committed by others (a twist on *ahimsa* developed by Thoreau, Tolstoy, Gandhi, and others); and (iii) finding alternative, creative ways to respond to violence. This third type of opposition is often the most surprising and rewarding part of opposing violence, and the part that has come to be emphasized by the social sciences and by helping professions such as counseling.

Not Committing Violence Ourselves

There are not very many statements that everyone in the world would agree on. But here is one candidate: "If everyone else were nonviolent, the world would be better than it is now."

Do you agree? Most people do. Would you be willing to go further and include yourself among those who should be nonviolent? Do you sense a bit of hesitation this time? Why?

Most of us commit at least small acts of violence occasionally. When we do, each of us is wired to see our own violence as justified. We say things all the time that reveal this self-justification, such as "She hit me first," "He had it coming," or "I had to teach him a lesson." These statements are not facts but rationalizations for a choice we made to be violent.

Usually when a person commits an act of violence, he or she justifies it in terms of self-protection or self-defense. I might be striking back at you in retaliation because you punched me in the nose. Or I might be part of an army invading your country — just as a precaution, before you can invade my country. Whether it is retaliatory or precautionary, I probably tell myself that the violence is necessary. It is necessary in order to protect myself from you harming me.

When harm is extended to include disrespect, I can construct a justification for resentment, hostility, and even physical violence in response to almost anything that makes me feel even slightly misused. Disrespect, the great common thread running through all acts of violence, pulls open the door to violence, by making my retaliation feel proper, and even necessary.

Nonviolence asks us to question this way of justifying our own violence. On the one hand, we consciously deplore violence and want to get rid of it: "There is just too much violence in the world today." Yet, almost instinctively, we reserve the right to be violent in our own defense: "But I'll hurt you if you try anything, buddy."

Now, if all violence can be justified in terms of self-defense, we have not moved anywhere. To break out of this pattern of thinking, we need to take responsibility for ending our own violence, acting in ways that discourage violence by others if possible, and looking for means other than violence to protect and defend ourselves.

Making the decision not to commit violence ourselves is very scary for most people. It feels like exposing ourselves to danger. Actually, this decision makes little or no difference in the external dangers that we usually face. However, deciding not to commit violence reduces the danger that we pose to others, and - because people tend to reap what they sow — reduces the likelihood that our behavior will provoke others to violence. Considering all the everyday forms of violence in which we might participate (just think of road rage), the decision not to commit violence ourselves can be an important step toward making our own world safer.

Not Cooperating with Violence Committed by Others

The large-scale violence of British colonial rule in India was the target of several noncooperation campaigns led by Gandhi. For example, in the "Salt Satyagraha" Indians defied the British salt monopoly by refusing to buy British salt and instead making their own. Similarly, Martin Luther King Jr. led campaigns of economic noncooperation against the abusive Jim Crow system of segregated public buses, restrooms, stores, and other public facilities in the southern United States. When these campaigns were illegal under the prevailing laws, they were by definition examples of civil disobedience.

Noncooperation with violence includes more than civil disobedience, however. One achievement of the women's movement over the past generation has been the creation of agencies and shelters where victims of domestic violence and sexual assault can find safety and assistance. The shelters and the movement that created them can be seen as a form of active noncooperation with intimate partner violence - a shameful plague that unfortunately is found all over the world.

The literature on noncooperation with governmental authority includes Henry David Thoreau's famous essay *Civil Disobedience*[31] and the Russian novelist Leo Tolstoy's writings[32] in opposition to militarism and the church's support of conscription under the Czars. The stance of conscientious objection to military service is an important and controversial type of noncooperation, but its more recent stories are little known publicly.[33]

Garden-variety bullying is close to home for most of us. Bullies get away with violence when we passively cooperate with them by remaining silent bystanders. Obviously one active approach would be to fight with the bully, a response of punitive violence. As we know, this is the response that many people advocate and promote.

But a student named Emily in one of our workshops envisioned another active approach. Emily believed that if a large percentage of the people in her high school knew about nonviolence, the peer pressure among students would then operate very differently. She imagined that if a bullying incident occurred in the hallway between classes, a crowd of students might converge immediately, telling the bully that violence is stupid and that the way to earn respect is to show respect. This would be active noncooperation with a common form of violence, but clearly it would require preparation in the form of comprehensive nonviolence education.

Schools should be asking not just how bullies should be punished, but how Emily's crowd of nonviolent students could become a natural feature of the school's culture.

Emily's insight was that, although there are many inspiring stories about individuals responding nonviolently in potentially violent situations, we should not ask individual nonviolence to perform miracles in the midst of a culture that is accustomed to passively cooperating with violence. Rather, we should use nonviolence education to change the culture so that it no longer provides nourishment to violence. For her, and for us, nonviolence training would be a step in that direction.

Creating Alternative Ways to Respond

Nonviolence doesn't work by somehow taking away the option of violence, which many people perceive as their most obvious means of self-defense. Rather, nonviolence seeks to provide better options than violence for achieving happiness and security. One of the pleasures of learning about nonviolence is discovering that there is more - much more - to nonviolence than simply "not using violence." There are hundreds of stories about nonviolence that are marked by moments of surprise, relief, humor, and unexpected discovery, as creative solutions are found to problems that had seemed doomed to violence. Consider this Civil Rights Movement story from David Halberstam's book *The Children*:[34]

The Nashville sit-in campaign of 1960, led by a group of black college students including Bernard LaFayette, the author of our Foreword, was the beginning of desegregation in that city. The nonviolence-trained students were frequently harassed by groups of young white men who resented the changes that were taking place.

One Saturday, a group of students was walking to a lunch counter demonstration when a gang of white men attacked them. A student named Solomon Gort was knocked down and was being beaten. LaFayette moved to protect Gort by covering him with his own body, whereupon the attackers turned their kicks and blows on Bernard.

The person who had been teaching nonviolent strategy to the students was Jim Lawson, a pastor who had come to Nashville at the urging of Martin Luther King precisely because Lawson had spent time in India studying Gandhi's legacy. Lawson calmly walked up to the beating of Gort and LaFayette, and the gang turned its attention to this new person. Lawson, cool and mature, wasn't fighting - but he was clearly interfering with their business.

The leader of the gang spat on Lawson. Lawson remained calm, and asked the leader for a handkerchief. A handkerchief was given, and Lawson wiped the spit off. Then, noting that the leader wore a leather jacket, Lawson asked him if he owned a motorcycle. He did. Some questions and answers about motorcycles followed, while in the background Gort and

LaFayette got to their feet and the students resumed their walk. Rejoining the students, Lawson waved at the gang leader, who just remained still, watching them go, and probably wondering what had just happened.

Our colleague Bernard LaFayette went on to join Dr. King's staff, and has become a beloved nonviolence educator in the King tradition. He was one of the eight "Children" who are the main focus of Halberstam's book about several young people who became first foot soldiers, and later veterans, of the Civil Rights Movement.

We will always be deeply moved by Jim Lawson's courage and creativity in the "motorcycle story." To us, this story is a good example of how nonviolence includes much more than just refraining from violence, and how it often involves surprise - a departure from the violent script that people have been expecting events to follow.

A key idea in the practice of nonviolence is that every situation offers us a range of ways in which to respond. Usually, some of these options will be more in the spirit of nonviolence than others, and so we can choose a response from the more nonviolent end of this spectrum. We may have difficulty seeing the range of options arrayed before us, perhaps because we have formed strong habits to respond in only one standard way. However, we can learn to see a wider range of options through study, discussion, openness to ideas that are not obvious, and sheer practice. For many people, it is a big step forward just to begin thinking about the existence of this range of options.

However, finding alternatives to violence does not necessarily depend on a head-scratching random brainstorming of logical possibilities. In the motorcycle story, it is important that Jim Lawson's way of transforming the danger of violence into a less threatening situation involved focusing on a human connection between adversaries. We can generalize from this example to say that many stories of nonviolence are stories about relationship-building. We can be pretty certain that the alternatives most likely to transform conflict peacefully are those that focus on human relationships.

2. Caring About Others

Increased caring about others is an outcome of nonviolence education that relates directly to the origin concept *agape*. Let's examine some of the ways in which caring manifests itself, and some of the specific obstacles to be overcome.

Author Charles Collyer, together with Abu Bakr, a nonviolence trainer and formerly Assistant to the President of the University of Rhode Island, devised an informal scale for rating the atmosphere in schools they visited. At the bottom of the scale were schools where, from the teachers and administrators, we would hear things like this: "These damn kids. They won't listen to a word you say. You can't turn your back on them. You guys better watch out. They'll manipulate you." At the other extreme were schools where we would hear things like this: "These are our kids. It's difficult for them these days. But they are good people. Listen to what they have to say. If you respect them, they will listen to you." What do you think it is like to be a student in schools at the top, and at the bottom, of this scale?

We can also imagine a scale that gives a rough measure of how much people care for other people in general. At the bottom would be sentiments like "Don't be a sucker. You can't trust anybody. People are no damn good." At the top would be "Human beings are endlessly fascinating, complex, and wonderful. We have our problems, but just look at what we can do, especially when we work together."

A friend of ours, the blues historian and musician James "Sparky" Rucker, points out that people have two eyes at the front of our heads, rather than one in front and one in back, or one on each side. This means, according to Sparky, that "we can't watch our own backs, so we were meant to look out for each other." Sparky, the gruff old blues guy, is at the top of our caring scale.

Some people really enjoy and like other people, and others do not. It is easier to teach the knowledge and skills of nonviolence to people who have a positive attitude toward others and believe in their potential to be friends and allies.

Such people start their own pilgrimage to nonviolence with a head start, because they already possess something that the best teachers of nonviolence always try to encourage.

Both Gandhi and King repeatedly spoke of human beings in a way that emphasized their positive potential. For example,

From Gandhi: "It is the law of love that rules mankind. Had violence [or hate] ruled us, we should have become extinct long ago. And yet the tragedy of it is that the so-called civilized men and nations conduct themselves as if the basis of society was violence. [35]

From King: "...man is neither innately good nor is he innately bad; he has potentialities for both."[36]

Notice that Gandhi and King are not saying that all people are good, period. They are saying that people are capable of both good and bad, and can choose love, justice, nonviolence, and goodness over their opposites.

Can learning about nonviolence improve my attitude toward other people? Evaluations of nonviolence training suggest that the answer is yes. More research needs to be done on this, but the process seems to work as follows:

Nonviolence seeks to find and support what is good in me. That support can make me feel good about myself, and give my self-respect a boost. Nonviolence also points out what is good in you. It can remind me that you deserve my respect too. It can motivate both of us to get to know each other, join forces to get bigger jobs done, find our common problems and work on them together, and help each other when one of us is down. In short, nonviolence leads us to care about each other by focusing attention on the positive common ground that we share with each other.

What prevents many of us from caring for others in this way? There are several forces that can work either for or against caring, including: cultural messages; how we build our identity; how we process our experiences with others; and our world-view or religion.

Cultural Messages

Many cultural messages support the opposite of caring. For the most part, our culture tells us to care for good people, but to punish bad people. So, before we care about other human beings, we are expected to decide which ones are good and which are bad. Many TV shows, movies, and video games encourage this perception of people as either good or bad. In a typical action movie, the villain is painted as unforgivably bad, and the audience builds up hatred and fear toward (usually) him. Then toward the end of the movie, when an avenging good guy is finally unleashed to make the bad guy suffer, the audience experiences this revenge as justice.

"Well," you might say, "some people commit bad deeds. Isn't it naïve to care about them? Won't that just reward and support more bad deeds?" Let us be clear that people who commit bad deeds must be held accountable for them. Nonviolence and responsibility are emphatically "joined at the hip." But nonviolence requires that we distinguish between two kinds of response: (1) holding others accountable for their behavior, and (2) acting out our own feelings toward them. The first is a proper basis for justice; the second is often anger-driven and irresponsible.

A caring and responsible attitude toward wrongdoers would make punishments fit the crime, avoiding personal injury and humiliation, and providing for as much restoration of damage and rehabilitation as possible. The goal should be to find and develop the best potential for good, not simply to satisfy our temporary craving for revenge. In a great deal of media entertainment however, revenge is equated with justice, and the idea of turning offenders into productive members of the community is barely considered.

It is one thing to be realistically prepared for self-serving and manipulative actions by others. People are not perfect, and we owe it to ourselves to avoid being abused. However, it is easy to go further and, forgetting all the good that can also be drawn out of people, conclude that suspicion should dominate our attitude toward others. A general good will toward others can coexist with reasonable precautions against abuse. We should consider how cultural messages can be created that would encourage this balance.

How We Build Our Identity

A colleague of ours, a college professor, had a disturbing experience. He had just finished a section of his course on the topic of tensions between different ethnic groups in American society, and had asked his students to write brief comments in reaction to this topic. One student wrote that she felt it was necessary for her to hate some other ethnic groups in order for her to "know myself as a member of my own group." This story suggests that identity, the sense of who we are, is defined not only in terms of positive characteristics that belong to us, but in terms of negative characteristics that are ascribed to others. Why would a person feel less well known to herself without someone to hate? The answer may lie in a commonplace but very powerful bit of human psychology:

The people, places, and things that we experience repeatedly, first become familiar to us, and eventually what is familiar comes to seem normal and even natural. When we encounter new people from backgrounds different than our own, and experience them - their speech, their customs, their most noticeable departures from what is familiar - as "not normal," it is then just a small step to become wary, suspicious, and prejudiced against them, because their unfamiliarity leaves us in a state of uncertainty about what to expect from them. In this almost automatic way, we can develop a collection of contrasting beliefs about Them (the strange, abnormal ones) and Us (the familiar, normal ones) that become part of our identity, our conception of who we are. We are clean; they are dirty. We are intelligent; they are stupid. We know how to behave; they don't. And so on. These thoughts about Them become excuses not to care about Them as fellow human beings, to further distance ourselves from Them, and therefore to crystallize our ignorance and unfamiliarity with Them. To fill the void, we may generate additional poorly grounded beliefs about Them that further distance Them and draw the boundaries between Them and Us even more sharply. This is a vicious cycle in which ignorance and false beliefs feed on each other.

Is there another way to build our identity, other than through negative contrasts with others? Certainly. First, we can be aware of how the experience-familiarity-normality chain works to create our prejudices. Many of the beliefs we arrive at are not objective facts about Them, but products of this chain and related thought processes.

Second, we can counteract these beliefs through better educating ourselves about the world outside our familiar sphere. Good information gathering will reveal that within any group of Them, there is tremendous variation among individuals. Once this is understood, it will render any blanket statements about whole ethnic or racial groups nonsensical.

Third, we can use these tools - awareness of our own thought processes, and meaningful education - to build our own identity on a solid foundation of knowledge about our own strengths and weaknesses, without lazily leaning on shallow overall comparisons with other groups.

How We Process Our Experiences with Others

We all have bad experiences with people. We all have good experiences too. However, memory and attention are selective. It is very easy to select our bad experiences to dwell on, and ignore the good ones. When we do this, we predictably shape our own attitude and mood to be persistently negative. This can set self-fulfilling prophecies into motion, in which the reactions we create through our bad attitude come back to us in the form of hostility and avoidance by other people. What stronger confirmation of our negative views could we get than the nasty hostility of our neighbors and co-workers? And yet, the source of that hostility was not in them, but in our own choice to focus on our own bad experiences. One consequence of this vicious cycle is that we come to care little for others, because we perceive them to be causing our own pain.

Selectivity and self-fulfilling prophecies work in the other direction too. If we select our best experiences with people to think about, that will influence our mood, speech, and actions in a positive way. And what goes around, comes around. Projecting a positive attitude usually influences the people around us to return the favor. It is then pretty easy to care about the welfare of those people, because they are being so good to us!

A balanced view of life recognizes that both good and bad things happen. It also recognizes that our own actions can become good or bad events in the lives of others as well as our own. (How often have I, through carelessness or otherwise, been a part of what someone else experiences as "Murphy's Law" - the proposition that whatever can go wrong, will go wrong?) There is much more to be said about all this. For the present, however, it is sufficient to note that our willingness to care for others is related to what we select and emphasize in processing our experiences with others.

World View or Religion

Liberating as it is to "let it go" and turn a problem over to a "higher power," this shift to the supernatural can also relieve us of our responsibility to others, and diminish caring about what happens in this world. The Serenity Prayer, attributed to Reinhold Niebuhr and widely used in self-help organizations such as Alcoholics Anonymous, expresses our need for a balance between accepting and acting: "Grant me the serenity to accept the things I cannot change, the courage to change the things I can, and the wisdom to know the difference." Too much emphasis on the first part can hold us back from caring. Too much emphasis on the second can make us a loose cannon. It really does take wisdom to know the difference.

Both Gandhi and King were religious men, but in a worldly way that made them different from some of the other leaders of their religions. Gandhi directed his Hindu followers away from supernatural fatalism. He emphasized what people could do in this life to free themselves and improve conditions for women and the "untouchables." King criticized other Christian ministers who emphasized getting to heaven upon death over improving social conditions for the living.

Like cultural messages, the building of identity, and the processing of our own experiences, our world-view or religion can either promote or inhibit caring for others. Learning about nonviolence nudges a person in the direction of caring, and so may transform how each of these factors operates in our lives.

3. Goal Orientation

We can analyze Goal-Orientation into at least two important ideas. One is the concept expressed beautifully in the phrase "Eyes on the Prize" – that we should resist being sidetracked in the pursuit of our most important goals; the other is the requirement that, in solving problems, our methods should be consistent with the goals we are pursuing.

Eyes on the Prize

The wonderful phrase "Eyes on the Prize" is the title of a video history of the Civil Rights Movement, produced by the Public Broadcasting System. The phrase comes from the determined refrain of the gospel freedom song "Hold On." Here is the last verse of the familiar Alice Wine version:

> Got my hand on the freedom plow,
> Wouldn't take nothin' for my journey now.
> Keep your eyes on the prize, hold on.
> Hold on, hold on!
> Keep your eyes on the prize, hold on.

Keeping our eyes on the prize means staying focused on our main goal. That is what Martin Luther King was doing that January evening in 1956 when he asked his angry friends to go home. This kind of goal orientation is the opposite of an automatic reflex; it is a skill, a way of thinking that must be learned. Stories like the one about Dr. King can help us to cultivate this skill and bring it closer to being our habitual way of operating.

In nonviolence, the skill of staying focused on what is really important is called upon when we must survive moments of anger which threaten to lead us into insulting, threatening, humiliating, or physically hurting others. These moments usually pass, and are followed by a calmer emotional state in which we are less inclined to hurt our "enemy" and more able to work nonviolently to solve our problems with him or her.

The song "Hold On" is part of the rich musical heritage of the Civil Rights Movement and its precursors. Its message - be patient, keep working for good, and keep the goal in mind - was a needed reminder to people who were assaulted daily by the taunts, cruelty, and abuse of the powerful, for years and years.

Actually, both King and Gandhi were often criticized for their patience in the face of this abuse. People are easily tempted into lashing back at those who hurt them. But in the long run, it became clear that the patience of these great leaders was a purposeful, restrained choice about how to respond. Their reputations were built by pressing a long-term struggle against injustice while refusing to be baited into short-term violence.

The old advice about moments of anger, that we should "count to ten" (or a hundred) in order to let anger pass, is good advice. But we should also understand that getting through these moments is not done just to demonstrate that we can do it. Staying under control helps us to achieve our goals. The advice would be more complete if it said "count to ten, and while you do, keep your eyes on the prize."

Consistency of Methods and Goals

Another theme that runs through both Gandhi's and Martin Luther King's writings is that our means (that is, our methods) should be consistent with our ends (that is, our goals). More exactly,

" ... nonviolence demands that the means we use must be as pure as the ends we seek." [37]

Now, think about this. Is Dr. King saying that "the end justifies the means"?

No, quite the contrary. The phrase "the end justifies the means" suggests that there is only one moral decision to make - that after we have chosen a good goal, any method for achieving it is then justified. But Dr. King is not saying that at all. Instead, he is saying that we need to make two moral decisions, not just one, and both must be good decisions.
We must choose both our ends and our means. Furthermore, we need to choose each of them nonviolently, so that the consistency achieved is one in which the means and the ends do not poison and undermine each other. The goodness of one component does not automatically carry over to the other, as implied by the "end justifies the means" claim. But badness does

carry over. We can undermine a good goal by choosing evil methods to attain it. And the surface goodness of our methods will be undermined if we use them to pursue an evil goal.

The consistency of methods and goals is another high standard to which we are held by nonviolence. The benefits that flow from consistency include, first, the quality of a person's reputation. A person who is recognized as being of good character is often one whose methods and goals are consistent with each other. Second, and perhaps more important, is that goals achieved through consistent nonviolent methods are not burdened with an embarrassing history of underhanded methods. They are more likely to be goals we can be proud of, and to be longer lasting.

An obvious objection must be stated: Our very ability to choose nonviolent methods is sometimes limited because of a past history of hostile actions and persistent avoidance of nonviolent problem-solving. For example, the Treaty of Versailles ending World War I was a punitive treaty that humiliated Germany and so bred resentment in that country against the Allies, fueling "enemy thinking" rather than defusing it. The failure to end World War I in a fair and compassionate way led twenty years later to World War II. It is commonly said that for the Allies, fighting World War II was necessary, because the goal of defeating Hitler was so important. Indeed, World War II does seem to be a case where the end justified the means, and is often used as an argument against nonviolence in general. What is often forgotten is that the violent means of war would not have been necessary if the problem represented by Hitler had been addressed through more pragmatic and less vindictive diplomacy twenty years earlier.

A great reason to practice nonviolence all the time, and not just in times of crisis, is to stay off the slippery slope that leads individuals and nations into violent conflict as the lesser of available evils.

(Paradoxically, the prevention of war escapes our attempts to study it, because what is prevented, by definition, never presents itself for study. This is a familiar dilemma for those who argue the merits of prevention in many domains of problem-solving - poverty, crime, public health, and the environment, to name a few.)

A more immediate and positive motive for practicing nonviolence all of the time is that everyday life is then more productive, satisfying, and fun. Happily, these benefits can be measured. And, incidentally, this kind of life prevents violence.

Of course, we must also be prepared for crisis, and for the use of extreme means if necessary. But we should not depend on creating violent man-made crises to keep us energized and ready to use these capabilities; there are always plenty of naturally occurring crises to do that. We should base our preparation and training on a realistic view of the world and of human nature, recognizing that however much we may wish for a placid existence with no crises, wishing alone won't make it real. The actual world in which we must live and take part ironically often forces us into struggle to achieve peace and freedom.

So, after achieving any measure of peace and freedom, it is unwise to relax, congratulate ourselves, and just coast. "Freedom isn't free," we hear politicians say. True. However, yet another irony is that this slogan is often used to justify wars that could have been prevented at much lower cost – prevented by acting in accordance with that very same slogan. A fair price for freedom is eternal nonviolent vigilance.

4. Facing Reality

The expression "facing reality" typically evokes one of two interpretations. It could be understood as passively accepting the real world with resignation, as in the remark, "You may as well face reality …" Or it could be understood as actively confronting the world as it really is, in order to solve real problems, instead of indulging in wishful thinking.

Here we are interested in the second, more active sense of "facing reality." Let us break this aspect of nonviolence into three components: acquiring accurate knowledge; facing unpleasant as well as pleasant facts; and adopting practical strategies and tactics.

Acquiring Accurate Knowledge

Nonviolence aims to create a better world. However, you can't improve something unless you have accurate knowledge about its current condition - that is, about its reality. In his *Letter from Birmingham Jail*, Martin Luther King said that the first step in any nonviolent campaign is "the collection of facts to determine whether injustices exist." In a larger sense, information gathering is the first responsibility of anyone who hopes to solve a problem.

There are typically two kinds of knowledge that we need: general background to build our understanding of the context, and specific information about the problem at hand.

We also need to have a good understanding of nonviolence itself, including its history, its philosophical variations, and a broad repertoire of examples. We need to understand human nature as well as possible, and with as much generosity and tolerance as we can muster. We need to know how the world works economically, politically, and technically, the pitfalls and problems that people can face, and ways of bringing help to bear. And we need to understand artistic expression - how people tell in language and music and visual images about the human condition.

These are reasons to commit to a life of continual learning and education. They are offered to anyone who is looking for a reason to stay in school, go back to school, to study research methods, or to start in on the study of a worthwhile subject.

Facing Unpleasant as well as Pleasant Facts

A practitioner of nonviolence should not be naïve. The world includes very harsh and unpleasant realities. The arenas in which nonviolence is most needed are environments in which ugly things happen. Women fear bodily injury and death at the hands of current and former lovers. High school students are victimized by bullying, drugs, gambling, and sexual predation. Gangs retaliate against each other in brutal ambushes. Co-workers manipulate and sabotage each other for advantage in the workplace. Salespeople tell outright lies dozens of times each day to maintain their incomes and their jobs. Arms dealers sell deadly weapons to both sides in wars around the world. This dreary and disgraceful list goes on and on.
There is no quick remedy for most of these problems. Nonviolence does not assume that we can solve difficult problems quickly, or that violent people can be turned around with just a few words. It does offer some insights however:

- Violence tends to occur as part of a cycle of mutual retaliation which we need to understand if we are to interrupt it.

- Likewise, violence especially pervades systems in which some people oppress and intimidate others.
- The perpetrators of violence are degraded by their own actions, and so suffer losses which we need to appreciate.
- The positive common ground that people share is easily pushed aside and forgotten in conflict. This loss of connection happens without conscious intent. However, re-establishing common ground takes deliberate effort and skill.
- In most conflicts, each side owns part of the truth. That is, each has a perspective on the problem that is rooted in real interests and needs. Therefore, we need to learn from both sides, even when some of the truth may be embedded in grave injustices.

Nonviolent leaders are sometimes criticized for their willingness to attribute some truths, some value, to an enemy hated by their followers. But one of the ways in which people avoid reality is by refusing to learn from people who are disliked and despised. We can obviously learn more if we do not avoid any information that can help us solve difficult problems.

Adopting Practical Strategies and Tactics

Gandhi and King were both skilled politicians. They made shrewd judgments every day about all the practical needs of their movements. They picked their battles carefully. They built support for difficult political tasks by bringing people from different classes and interest groups together. Their success was grounded in facing the facts of each situation and working with the real interests and limitations of the people who were involved. The changes they brought about could not have been accomplished if these leaders had been naïve or impractical men.

However, in a critique of Gandhi's nonviolence, the theologian Reinhold Niebuhr (whom King greatly admired) made a distinction between Gandhi's attempts to deal with others out of a spirit of good will, and his political methods. He described the first as a loving attitude:

"Non-violence, for him, has really become a term by which he expresses the ideal of love, the spirit of moral goodwill. This involves for him freedom from personal resentments and a moral purpose, free of selfish ambition. It is the temper and spirit in which a political policy is conducted … rather than a particular political technique." [38]

Physically nonviolent political action, however, like violent methods, according to Niebuhr, is not neutral but coercive:

"Non-violent coercion and resistance, in short, is a type of coercion which offers the largest opportunities for a harmonious relationship with the moral and rational factors in social life." [39]

Though the young Martin Luther King was at first somewhat taken aback by Niebuhr's characterization of nonviolence as a form of coercion, he was definitely inspired by the conclusion of Niebuhr's argument (written 25 years before the Montgomery Bus Boycott) as it related to black people in America:

"This means that non-violence is a particularly strategic instrument for an oppressed group which is hopelessly in the minority and has no possibility of developing sufficient power to set against its oppressors. The emancipation of the Negro race in America probably waits upon the adequate development of this kind of social and political strategy. It is hopeless for the Negro to expect complete emancipation from the menial social and economic position into which the white man has forced him, merely by trusting in the moral sense of the white race. It is equally hopeless to attempt emancipation through violent rebellion." [40]

Both as a student and throughout his career, King must have read this prophetic passage of Niebuhr's again and again.

Was nonviolence used coercively by Gandhi, and later by King? The short answer must be yes. Nonviolence has often been used to pressure political and economic powers to "do the right thing." Consider this passage from the *Letter from Birmingham Jail*, written by a more seasoned Dr. King:

"You may well ask: 'Why direct action? Why sit-ins, marches, and so forth? Isn't negotiation a better path?' You are quite right in calling for negotiation. Indeed this is the very purpose of direct action. Nonviolent direct action seeks to create such a crisis and foster such a tension that a community which has constantly refused to negotiate is forced to confront the issue. It seeks so to dramatize the issue that it can no longer be ignored. My citing the creation of tension as part of the work of the nonviolent resister may sound rather shocking. But I must confess that I am not afraid of the word 'tension.' I have earnestly opposed violent tension, but there is a type of constructive, nonviolent tension which is necessary for growth." [41]

Here we see clearly King's view of nonviolence as a strong and active force, capable of grappling with difficult real-world problems. This view contrasts sharply with the assumption held by many people that nonviolence is a passive or resigned attitude, averse to tension or confrontation.

The strategies and tactics of nonviolence have, for the most part, been developed by disadvantaged people. Its practitioners – in South Africa, India, the United States, the Philippines, Chile, and many other places - were not able to get what they wanted by physical force, great wealth, or raw political power. So they devised ways for relatively powerless people to exert pressure for change in other ways. The invention of nonviolent political action deserves a place in any list of examples of human progress.

5. Personal Investment

Personal investment means the effort and time and sacrifice that each of us puts in to become more nonviolent. Like nonviolence itself, personal investment takes many forms and is related to many other ideas. Let us approach this aspect of nonviolence by considering first the goals of personal investment, and then the methods that move us toward these goals.

Goals

There are two broad goals of personal investment: (1) personal development or empowerment, and (2) becoming a more effective agent of social change. There is actually some conflict between those who emphasize personal empowerment as an outcome of nonviolence, and those who see such empowerment as secondary to, and even a distraction from, the goal of agency for social change. We regard both personal development and agency for social change as worthwhile goals. Each provides a good reason for personal investment, and there is no necessary reason for them to be in conflict with each other. Rather, they should complement each other.

Almost all supporters of nonviolence would agree that individual human beings have an obligation to be instruments of positive change. To become more effective instruments, they should make a personal investment of time and energy to learn and practice the skills of nonviolence. The personal investment itself can be rewarding, and so can become one of the attractions of nonviolence. Many good programs for youth, including nonviolence training programs, can promise greater pride, confidence, and a sense of empowerment as beneficial outcomes.

Ironically, it is also desirable for a practitioner of nonviolence to be capable of violence. To abstain from violence only because one is too weak to use it, doesn't really count as nonviolence. Better is to be capable of violence, but choose nonviolent options deliberately and consistently. Therefore, one goal of personal development can be to become strong in the ways usually associated with violence. For example, martial arts training, especially in philosophically nonviolent disciplines such as aikido, has been chosen by many individuals as part of their personal investment in nonviolence.[42]

There is room for a great deal of variation in the goals adopted by different individuals. In a living tradition like nonviolence, we think it is quite proper for tastes and preferences to come into play. Also, life is not long enough to become a master of every skill, field of knowledge, art, or vocation. The value we place on personal growth itself, and the process of growing toward our goals, are more important than the particular discipline or level of skill we may attain.

Methods

Personal investment should probably include a daily program or regimen, in which development toward our goals receives some deliberate attention. Some people are naturally inclined toward such programs, and are strict about them. Others are more casual. Again, there is room for variation.

Gandhi is the most famous example of a nonviolent leader trying to practice everything he preached, starting with his own personal choices and routines. In Gandhi's case, personal investment took the form of giving up material possessions, alcohol, meat, sex, and many ordinary sources of comfort. His fasts, originally undertaken to put political pressure on his followers and opponents, also became a voluntary form of personal self-purification. He believed that his own life would inevitably be viewed as an example to others of nonviolence. Therefore, he wanted to ensure that people could learn about nonviolence by observing him. He also wanted to gain the political advantage of being seen as a poor and humble citizen-leader.

However, he had a wonderful sense of humor about the symbolic side of his asceticism: in the movie Gandhi we hear his acknowledgment that it cost a great deal of his supporters' money to keep him in poverty!

Many people, using Gandhi as their example, recoil from the self-sacrifice that they assume nonviolence requires. But, in fact, there are no "nonviolence police" out there checking up on our degrees of personal investment to ensure that they are adequate! Supporters of nonviolence cover quite a wide range on the dimension of personal investment, from relatively high, such as Gandhi-like self-denial, to relatively low, such as simply holding positive attitudes toward nonviolence among those whose lifestyles are more typical.

Reading about nonviolence, talking about it with others, and devoting time to hands-on applications of nonviolence, are all forms of personal investment that are accessible and worthwhile. Spending time in these ways has the direct benefit of building our understanding. It also brings the indirect benefit of enriching the rest of our time. As the saying goes, "What's not to like?"

In Conclusion

We have examined five aspects of nonviolence - five varieties of discovery that we have observed in people who are learning about the details of nonviolence for the first time. One of the aspects - opposition to violence - is couched in a semantically negative way. The other four - caring for others, goal-orientation, facing reality, and personal investment - are couched positively.

In the end, the positive or negative phrasing of these aspects when briefly stated, is their least important feature. It is clear to everyone who does a little study that nonviolence is a positive and powerful concept. However, the negative valence of the term nonviolence itself may be partly responsible for the relatively poor understanding that so many people have of this powerful idea.

There is nothing fixed or sacred about the five aspects of nonviolence presented here. The purpose of discussing these aspects has simply been to stimulate your interest in nonviolence by opening up and laying out some of its richness for inspection.

When Dr. King spoke to his followers after the bombing of his home in Montgomery, he personified nonviolence for them, and dramatically turned them away from committing violence. His example broadened their view of nonviolence, and ultimately confirmed for the crowd that Dr. King's approach was the one they wanted.
Consider what it must have been like to be a member of that crowd of angry friends. That was a real, powerful moment in time for them. Their emotions ran high. Before Dr. King spoke to them, they were about to go out and repeat a mistake that vengeful people have made millions of times before in human

history, a mistake that has usually resulted only in further hostility and destruction. But in that moment, the crowd heard a voice of reason, compassion, and quietly confident leadership, using that very moment to guide them and to teach a critically important lesson. That moment made all the difference. The world needs more moments turned to good purpose like that one. If more people become educated in nonviolent problem-solving, there will be more of us who are able to do what Dr. King did that night.

Nonviolence has multiple though related facets, and can challenge a person with its unfamiliarity as well as its complexity, its scariness, its combination of idealism and practicality, its connection to many different problems and fields, its applicability to difficult problems, and its very colorful literature.

We hope you will discover more about nonviolence through further exploration, and then - most importantly - pass on this understanding to others.

Chapter 5 - Making Nonviolence Real

One often hears the criticism that nonviolence is commendably idealistic, but not realistic. So this chapter is concerned with realism. To what extent can nonviolence be made real in the world, and what does it look like when it is realized?

We have presented many examples of nonviolence and approximations to nonviolence throughout *Discovering Nonviolence* and its companion, *Agape and Ahimsa*. We hope that these examples and approximations have provided a glimpse of the inclusive or "big tent" conception of nonviolence. We hope readers will see in these cases a kind of nonviolence that is robust and practical in real life.

However, there are two "reality issues" that we should discuss more fully and directly. One is a concern of scientists and policy makers: the issue of measurable outcomes. The other is a concern of professions charged with using force: the practicality of nonviolence in the face of violent threats.

Measurable Outcomes

For the most part, when we have spoken of the "outcomes" of nonviolence in this book, we have meant changed attitudes toward other people and toward problem-solving. We have described these changes in words and stories rather than in statistical terms. For most social scientists, however, the measurability of outcomes is paramount. And in the disciplines concerned with human services and organizational development there is a branch of applied social science called program evaluation, which uses rigorous methodology to test for the existence of real effects of educational and other programs. This book is not a guide to research on the effects of nonviolence education. However, abundant research does exist in fields such as psychology and education, and advanced study in nonviolence should include this literature. There are studies of the basic psychological processes that underlie aggressive and prosocial behavior. There are also applied "outcome studies" in which the impact of particular programs and interventions is documented. This research is rich in ideas related to nonviolence and evidence for the effectiveness of nonviolence education broadly construed. The research literature is too large to be reviewed in this book, but we would like to offer some entry points to this information that we believe will make an immediate connection for the reader between our account of nonviolence and empirical research. Here are some suggestions:

A classic paper on children's imitation of aggressive behavior was published by Albert Bandura and colleagues.[43] This study demonstrated that children would copy the behavior and the words of an adult role model who was observed punching and yelling at an inflatable "Bobo doll." Young children were more likely to imitate if the role model was of their own gender, and boys were overall more aggressive than girls. The study was of theoretical importance because the researchers did not provide obvious rewards to the children for engaging in aggressive behavior. Rather, the children picked up the behavior simply by watching. Many research studies by psychologists followed, examining aspects of modeling and imitation, including the effects of watching violence on television. Bandura's famous Bobo doll study serves here as an example of important research on the basic conditions and psychological processes involved in problematic violent behavior.

A review article by David Johnson and his brother Roger Johnson provides an example of scholarship focused on the effectiveness of programs to reduce violence.[44] These authors reviewed the available literature on conflict resolution and peer mediation programs in schools. They concluded that, while the research was incomplete and problematic, several conclusions could be drawn:

a. Conflicts among students do occur frequently in schools (although the conflicts only rarely result in serious injury).
b. Untrained students by and large use conflict strategies that create destructive outcomes by ignoring the importance of their ongoing relationships.

c. Conflict resolution and peer mediation programs do seem to be effective in teaching students integrative negotiation and mediation procedures.

d. After training, students tend to use these conflict strategies, which generally leads to more constructive outcomes.

e. Students' success in resolving their conflicts constructively tends to reduce the number of student-student conflicts referred to teachers and administrators, which in turn, tends to reduce suspensions.

Johnson and Johnson focused on conflict resolution and peer mediation programs, which we place under the "big tent" of nonviolence education programs. What about programs with other labels and vocabularies for putting what we call nonviolence into practice? Daniel Goleman, in his book *Emotional Intelligence*, provides an appendix called "Social and Emotional Learning: Results."[45] In it he identifies several nonviolence-like programs which have had empirically validated outcomes, with source references. The concerns addressed by these programs include child development, social competence, awareness, problem-solving, and resolving conflict creatively.

One study that directly examined the impact of Kingian nonviolence training on the knowledge and attitudes of several groups who participated in two-day workshops, was done by Maram Hallak in 2000. Dr. Hallak found changes in knowledge and attitudes that lasted for months after the workshops.[46]

Another study showed that brief nonviolence training increases a person's sensitivity to violence, defined as how violent the person considers each of several violent behaviors to be.[47] Even the mere suggestion that an act of violence was justified or unjustified can, under some conditions, change how violent it is considered to be, illustrating how malleable human perceptions of violence are.[48] There are marked individual differences in baseline levels of sensitivity to violence.[49] However, changes in sensitivity are possible for both more sensitive and less sensitive individuals. Reasonably enough, nonviolence is associated with higher levels of awareness of the harm done by both outright violence and by lower levels of mean-spirited behavior.

We believe that these studies reflect a basic truth about teaching peaceful problem-solving: that nonviolence works. Its effectiveness has been demonstrated over and over again in the research literature. One approach to demonstrating a program's effectiveness is called meta-analysis, in which a systematic review of many research studies is undertaken. In this approach, a large number of studies on a type of treatment are collected, and the results are pooled statistically to create a more powerful test of the treatment's effect. Mark Lipsey and David Wilson carried out a meta-analysis that demonstrated the effectiveness of several kinds of psychological, educational, and behavioral treatments using a variety of outcome measures. To cite only some of the results related to nonviolence education, the paper documents effects in such categories as primary prevention education programs, social skills training, social learning treatment and diversion programs for juvenile delinquents, training in interpersonal cognitive problem-solving skills for children, assertiveness training, and guidance and counseling programs. The treatment effects in these categories were found to be moderate in size - not huge, but not trivial either. In other words, these are programs worth designing, investing in, and implementing; however, they should not be expected to produce dramatic or immediate change in every individual.[50]

A later review of over 200 socio-emotional learning (SEL) programs involving more than a quarter of a million school children, confirmed that SEL promotes not only positive social and emotional behavior but higher academic achievement.[51] (The emergence of good measures of SEL effects has tempted some school systems to begin using these measures not as tools to encourage progress in character development, but high-stakes tests to rank schools and punish low-performing teachers. Angela Duckworth, a leading researcher on SEL and character development, is among those resisting this more "violent" application of our new knowledge about the importance of nonviolence.)[52]

A great many other studies could be cited. The research supporting nonviolence education constitutes a strong empirical foundation for the development of programs aimed at teaching the skills of nonviolence. In a way, the social science research community has followed Gandhi's advice to experiment with nonviolence, to refine it and develop it further. Of course, we still need to translate what we know about nonviolence more fully into real life. And we need to keep studying and experimenting with new ways to create peace, and to train future generations to continue this work.

Nonviolence in the Face of Violent Threats

The attacks of September 11, 2001 set off a great many discussions about how people should respond to violence. The attacks were extreme, and the deliberate killing of innocent people has been almost universally condemned – a tragic point of agreement throughout the months and years of public debate. There was also a general agreement – so general that it is rarely stated – that people want their leaders' responses to terrorism to make the situation better rather than worse. However, people have disagreed over whether particular responses, such as military counterattack, or specific forms of counterattack, are necessary or unnecessary, and whether they would actually make things better or worse.

Shortly after September 11, there were several sharp criticisms of nonviolence from commentators who took the position that the attacks provided a clear instance in which violent counterattack was justified, and where a nonviolent approach would obviously be inadequate. These commentators made the usual assumption that "nonviolence" means a passive acceptance of wrongdoing. Given that the acknowledged icons of nonviolence, Gandhi and King, gave us powerful examples of how to strike down injustice, it is remarkable that this assumption persists. We trust that readers of this book now understand that real nonviolence vigorously seeks alternatives to both violence and passivity in the face of threats, conflicts, and frustrating problems in general. As Walter Wink has said, it is a third path. Nonviolence is a way of facing reality rather than avoiding it or lashing out.

The authors of this book share the disdain for passivity expressed by those commentators who, we feel mistakenly, set out after September 11 to protect the world from nonviolence. However, as teachers of active nonviolence, the post-attack debates placed us under considerable pressure to explain our position. The pressure has come from both those whose readiness to resort to violence is high, and from others who simply hold the familiar misconceptions of what nonviolence is all about.

There is an approach to the justification of violence, called Just War Theory (JWT), which is often cited as setting limits on nonviolence by saying when war is justified. Let us offer a perspective on JWT from the viewpoint of nonviolence. Then we will consider how a commitment to nonviolence can be brought into several very difficult areas of application. Our aim is to show how nonviolence would look, and sometimes does look, in the real world.

Just War Theory proposes conditions under which a country is justified in going to war. Scaled down, it addresses the more general question of when a person is justified in using force to solve a problem.

JWT proposes that war is justified under the following conditions: it is fought by a legitimate authority; it is fought for a just cause; it is fought as a last resort after other alternatives have been exhausted; and it is fought by ethical means. JWT also includes the traditional principles of discrimination and proportionality. Discrimination means that military personnel and resources, but not innocent civilians, may be targeted for attack. In warfare, imperfect discrimination is acknowledged to lead to some civilian casualties, a result euphemistically called collateral damage. Too much collateral damage may be considered "out of proportion" in any particular action, or for a war as a whole. Proportionality calls for the unwelcome judgment of how much damage is acceptable and how much is unacceptable. It can be seen that JWT offers a weighing of costs and benefits, both for war itself and for actions within a war.[53]

Another way to view JWT is that it is one approach to the setting of a threshold for violence. If a person or country has a low threshold, they will fight their perceived adversary on very little provocation. If the threshold is higher, this means that they would need to be provoked more strongly, or that they would wait longer before engaging in violence against their adversary. The existence of thresholds for violence, which vary from person to person, and which may even be expected to vary from time to time within any one person, is not very controversial. It is in fact a realistic way to view violence. Ira

Zepp conceded in his dialogue with Bill Holmes (see the Epilogue to *Agape and Ahimsa*) that he was aware of having a threshold, although for him it was very high ("on a scale of 1-10, I'd be something in the area of 9+.") Gandhi had a threshold, acknowledged in his example of the mad man running amok in a community, who would have to be stopped. Walter Wink admitted to being a violent man trying to get better – that is, to raise his threshold for violence.

Nonviolence aims to raise the threshold for violence, and hopefully to raise it so high that violence never occurs. But it uses alternatives to violence, constructive problem-solving skills, and *agape*, both to raise the threshold and to fill the space then available with other alternatives and options. Nonviolence goes beyond Just War Theory by proposing that, if we practice our skills of peacemaking and creative problem-solving, we may obviate the need for violence. It suggests that it is our responsibility as human beings to make sure that the conditions justifying war are never satisfied.

Is this idealistic? In one sense, yes. But, seen as a completely different attitude, nonviolence has very practical application in everyday affairs, from the personal level to the global. Nonviolence is about moving people from a position where their attention is focused on when they might have to fight, to a position where their attention is focused on adding more peaceful problem-solving to the world, so that there are fewer things to fight about. In this book we have described many of the skills of nonviolence that sometimes operate near the threshold where violence is about to begin. But more often we have been exploring ideas about how to work preventively, further below the threshold, where "ordinary life" takes place.

Now, it is reasonable to assume that we will not always succeed in pushing the threshold of violence out of reach. Most advocates of nonviolence would accept the idea that, in extreme circumstances, force will become necessary to solve a problem. The September 11 example often cited in this regard is Flight 93, the hijacked plane that crashed in the Pennsylvania countryside. Apparently, the passengers on that plane took violent action against the hijackers, and in doing so prevented the destruction of government targets in Washington, DC. Would we have wanted those passengers, in the name of nonviolence, not to have risen up against the men who had taken control of the plane? No. In such circumstances, violent action to prevent even greater violence may be the only option available to people of good will. The problem is that people so often resort to violence while they still have other options available to them.

Advocates of nonviolence observe that Just War Theory is often used to rationalize violence. Paul Robinson's article "Willing to kill but not to die," on the NATO bombing of Kosovo, is a powerful critique of the tendency of military powers to claim that the criteria of JWT have been satisfied, when in fact they have not, or when the question is at least still debatable. The implication is disturbing: rather than guarding against violence until certain conditions are met, JWT is available to the violence-prone, and to those trying to make up their minds, as an excuse for engaging in violence.

As we have noted previously, virtually every act of violence is justified in the mind of the violent actor as some kind of self-defense or legitimate response to threat, and therefore is felt to be necessary, at least for the moment. In nonviolence education, we are sometimes asked why we do not place more emphasis on proper ways to defend oneself. We try not to over-emphasize self-defense and other justifications, because people do not lack excuses for violence; quite the contrary – this is an area where human beings are already abundantly endowed. Highlighting self-defense keeps people thinking in old defensive, adversarial, reactive ways. Nonviolence represents a new way of thinking, not only about threat, but about all the times between threats.

All of us do need alternative approaches to dealing with threat. Nonviolence offers a range of alternatives to the usual "fight or flight" dichotomy. This is not to say that nonviolence will always work as intended. But tragically, for lack of a guarantee that it will work in the face of threat, nonviolence is seldom put to the test. Also, we easily forget that violence almost never works as we imagine it will; in fact, violence should be seen as a signal of failure to solve problems successfully.

So, what are some examples of nonviolent thinking in response to threat? Here are a few suggestions out of a vast repertoire of possibilities, ranging from the commonplace to the unexpectedly creative:

Consider the portion of the truth owned by your enemy. Consider the contribution that you may be making to the problem. Ask whether you have, and want, all the facts. Make an unexpected human gesture that transforms the situation. Invite your opponent to tea. "Send in a thousand grandmothers."[54] Refuse to insult and demean. Apologize. Talk, don't run away. Clearly state what you think is just, because maybe your enemy doesn't know. Grant amnesty. Provide constructive work. Offer a better deal. Ask your enemy to decide on a fair settlement, and then accept it. Build the opponent a school or hospital. Resist denial; accept that the situation is complicated and difficult. Forgive. Ask for mediation. Send a gift. Recall when you were friends, and stop calling him or her evil. Remove a threat that you hold over your enemy. Refuse to hate. Accept the decision of an arbitrator. Let it go. Go for life imprisonment rather than the death penalty. Support restorative justice over retribution. Say thank you. Regard violence as your real enemy. Be the one to stop the cycle of mutual humiliation, injury, and destruction. Find a way to be partners. Escape from the trap of enemy thinking. Consider *agape*. Consider *ahimsa*.

These options and strategies are often uncomfortable. But they often work. They have a much better track record than violence. We believe in these nonviolent options as realistic alternatives to violence. We feel that human beings too often fall into the trap of believing that the time for violence has come, when in fact there are still many practical options available for solving problems peacefully and creatively. At the same time, we do not minimize the difficulty of taking the nonviolent approach. While better outcomes are more likely with nonviolence, the resistance to reaching out in these ways to our adversaries can be paralyzing. Learning better how to overcome this paralysis is one of the major tasks ahead for nonviolence education.

On the question of whether nonviolence is sometimes necessary or inevitable, we remain open-minded. The logical necessity for violence has never been proven definitively. But examples like Flight 93 suggest that there are times, with time short and an emergency at hand, when our options are gone. We accept that those times do come, and acknowledge that they would satisfy JWT criteria. But we emphasize that such extreme cases are not good guides to action most of the time.

More work is needed to define the threshold for using force. JWT represents some of that work, and we grant that it has been well-intentioned. However, (1) JWT diverts attention and energy from adding more peace to the world; it focuses on the conditions under which we can permit ourselves to fail, rather than the activities that would enable us to succeed. Furthermore, (2) experience shows that JWT is used quite often to lower the threshold for going to war rather than to raise it; that is, it plays into our instinct to fight rather than holding us back from fighting.

The work of active nonviolence is not just to avoid violence, but to add peace – to promote work, fun, love, learning, and self-expression rather than violence. Making the world a more peaceful place is inherently worthwhile, and has the incidental side-effect of raising the threshold for violence.

Nonviolence and Law Enforcement

If acts of terrorism are crimes, then fighting them is a job for legitimate law enforcement and a properly constituted judicial system. These institutions are charged with the responsibility to use force in the defense of society when necessary. What does law enforcement look like when it is informed and motivated by nonviolence?

A friend of ours, Richard Tarlaian, is a skilled nonviolence trainer. He is also a retired senior officer of the Providence RI Police Department with a strong commitment to good community policing. It is part of a police officer's job to talk with members of the public, to confront suspicious persons, to mediate disputes, to make arrests, and so on. In practice, officers have a certain latitude in performing these duties. They can be courteous and firm in their dealings with others, or demeaning and provocative. They can exhibit respectful behavior that lays a foundation for future relationships, or they can sow seeds of continuing hostility and resentment. When dealing with someone suspected of a crime, often someone distrustful of him and disrespectful toward police in general, Richard would remind himself to ask the excellent question, "Does this situation need another jerk?" And the answer, unsurprisingly, would be "No." The question and the answer are a form of anger management. They became Rich's way of managing his own emotions and behavior in difficult, often angry, situations. In this way he could at least prevent himself from magnifying the problem at hand.

Here is another question Captain Tarlaian would ask himself: "What if I need this guy to be my ally next week?" This question is a reminder that today's adversaries may become tomorrow's partners – an evolution of events and relationships that happens all the time. In the heat of a given moment, we may lose sight of another person's capacity to help us in the future. But nonviolence provides a framework for remembering practical truths that our emotions often hide from us. Richard Tarlaian's approach to policing is both realistic and informed by nonviolence.

Here's a problem: Many people who identify themselves as peace advocates want nothing to do with the police. They identify the police as oppressors who maintain the power of the status quo. The do not subscribe to this kind of adversarial rhetoric. It is certainly true that police departments are the source of many horror stories regarding the use of violence and intimidation against less powerful people. These stories ought to be instructive examples of what to avoid. But we have seen many good police officers who, by nurturing young people toward more constructive lives, and in many other ways, contribute tangibly to addressing society's problems. We want peace advocates to be problem solvers and not blind critics of all police.

A strong reason for advocates of nonviolence to build and maintain good relations with their local police is that the police (and the military) can sometimes become allies in bringing about positive changes in society. Sharon Nepstad[55] concluded, after a review of several successful and unsuccessful attempts in different countries to stage nonviolent revolutions, that in most successful cases, the police eventually joined forces with the revolutionaries and refused to attack them. This kind of alliance is obviously more likely to occur, whether at the international or the local level, if the agents of nonviolent social change have an ongoing constructive relationship with the police than if they don't.

Consideration of policing and law enforcement invites an important question: What is the difference between force and violence? That is, are there some uses of force that lie below the threshold of violence? If so, then we want the legitimate use of force to be in a police officer's job description, but we would still want to keep "violence" out.

The difference between just force and unjust violence is illuminated by our examination of nonviolence in this book. Martin Luther King offered a simple and compelling definition of justice as that which uplifts the human personality, and of injustice as that which degrades it. With the job description of police officers, or with any other human relationship in need of definition, we can make good use of King's approach. Many effective police officers value human personality, respect their fellow citizens, and look beyond the present moment toward the needs of tomorrow when dealing with difficult characters. They are in line with King's definition of justice, and with the practical ideal of nonviolence. It is not easy, but that can also be said of nonviolence in general.

In many jurisdictions today, the professional training received by officers in police academies acknowledges the values of respect and human rights. These values also agree with and are strengthened by the personal beliefs of many individual officers. A continuing task for police training will be to present these values within a larger framework that motivates and educates all officers to perform their duties as confidently and nonviolently as possible.

As a society, we have not outgrown our need for the police. The question is what kind of policing we will demand, and support.

Nonviolence in Corrections

Prisons embody society's overriding desire to avoid the problems of crime and violence. The goal of *solving* these problems often seems secondary to this desire for avoidance. Offenders are sent away because they have literally offended us – made us angry, fearful, and vengeful. We think we will teach them a lesson. Of course, during their incarceration inmates often learn lessons that run counter to what we intended. Once they are behind bars we tend to neglect them, rather than invest in turning them around. (It must be said that many professionals in the field of corrections would have it otherwise.) In other words, we leave the imprisoned to spend their time with and be further educated by precisely the people we most fear and despise. This approach to "corrections" seems designed not to correct but to exacerbate violent criminal behavior. Society has chosen a hostile, adversarial approach which guarantees that it will continue to be plagued by violence. What could be further from the spirit of nonviolence?

To make things worse, our mandatory minimum sentences for even low-level violations of questionable laws, and the racially discriminatory application of these laws, has resulted in a rapid expansion of the U.S. prison population to between two and three million people. It is as if we were trying to turn people into criminals, rather than into fully functioning citizens.

There are many organizations working to reform society's approach to the organization of prisons, the irrational aspects of the law, and judicial philosophy in general. We cannot review all these efforts here, but we applaud them. Corrections is an important arena in which to pursue our best practices for promoting personal change. Perhaps surprisingly to some, nonviolence programs and other forms of educational programming are very welcome in many prisons, and receive a positive response from a large proportion of administrators, staff, and inmates.

Nonviolence in the Military

If we can conceive of nonviolent law enforcement and prison work, or approximations to them, what about the military? A nonviolent military at first seems to be the ultimate contradiction in terms. Yet, if we are to consider extending nonviolence into the most threatening real situations, and into the work of people charged with wielding a truly awesome potential for violence, this is exactly what we must consider.

First, it may be helpful to reconceptualize military action in terms of law enforcement rather than war. If nonviolence can influence the use of force in policing, the same principles may well carry over to national defense. One can discern moves in this direction over the past century, at least in the rhetoric used to describe and justify the use of military force. The Korean War was called a police action. The United States is said to play the role of the world's policeman. And so on. However, a serious reframing of the role of the military as enforcing the law may be helpful. For one thing, the principle of proportionality seems to be observed more carefully in the work of most law enforcement agencies than in the work of war. "Collateral damage" is not accepted and swept under the rug in police work as it often is in war. Strategies for minimizing violence and destruction are more central to policing, which takes place in the community, than in war, which if possible is carried out in the enemy's community. So, a shift away from large-scale violence toward a more measured use of force might begin with thinking of the military's job in terms of law enforcement, and imagining what that would look like.

Nonviolence has its own forms of fighting, and we have discussed many of them in this book. The activist Bernard LaFayette Jr. embraces the metaphor of nonviolent warriors, trained to fight injustice. The Montgomery bus boycott has been described as a nonviolent war, and its veterans, when they gather, have all the *esprit de corps,* and recapture all the past camaraderie, of any veterans' organization. Today there are Peace Brigade groups, which interpose themselves in zones of conflict, and there are proposals to create national or international military units to do the same. The military do not always need to go to war. They can also go to keep peace, and work to prevent war using the large repertoire of skills that nonviolence requires and teaches.

Military force is an instrument of a nation's foreign policy, and so we should also re-imagine the role of nonviolence in foreign affairs. Sadly, countries often do not practice the same values internationally that they espouse at home. A nation may stand for democracy, freedom, and self-determination, and yet its foreign policy may have the effect of denying these rights to other people through interference in elections, support for ruthless dictators, and other forms of diplomatic violence. A good start toward a nonviolent foreign policy for the United States would be to consistently promote its own ideals, rather than their opposites, overseas. Then it would be more likely that a proper role for the U.S. military in this dangerous world could be agreed upon.

Large-Scale Nonviolence in History

It may be true, as Walter Wink has said, that the world is not ready for real nonviolence. However, it must be ready for whatever it <u>is</u> ready for – that is, for the steps that can be taken in this generation to move us toward nonviolence. We need to think of nonviolence in broad, relative, and practical terms if we are to take these steps, because they will not necessarily look like "pure" nonviolence.

Actually, history provides quite a few examples of large-scale nonviolence – democracy, laws, courts, human service programs, education. Over time, the impact of these forms of nonviolent problem solving has tended to increase. For example, the voting franchise in the United States has expanded steadily from a few white men, to former slaves, to women, and finally to 18-year-olds. Higher education was once the privilege of only a few, but now is the expectation of about half the population. In just the past generation, shelters for victims of domestic violence have grown and spread in the United States to provide a wonderful example of a nonviolent response to a problem of violence in society. The shelters are not places of pure pacifism; they are very hands-on, nuts-and-bolts, practical problem-solving places. But two generations ago they hardly existed.

Viewed in this way, there has been progress toward a more nonviolent world. However, the word nonviolence is usually not associated with these examples. We wonder why, and we invite you to re-examine what nonviolence really means, with these examples in mind.

In the Final Analysis

If we are successful in building a peaceful world – a good world of work and love and fun and fellowship and fulfilling self-expression – it will not feel like "violence prevention." But, incidentally, it will be so.

This feature of nonviolence, that when it is successful it makes the thought of violence recede and the word nonviolence itself seem less relevant because of its etymology, is frustratingly ironic. It is as if during every period of daylight we forgot about the phenomenon of darkness. When violence is out of sight, it is kept out of mind by powerful forces of avoidance and denial. New ways of thinking are necessary both to build a peaceful world, and to hold forgetting at bay in the process.

We have a new paradigm to teach, a third path to replace the old dichotomy of complacency and violence. This third path is, as Gandhi said, is not really so new; he said that it was as old as the hills. It only seems new each time it is rediscovered. Nonviolence continues to be reborn century after century, with new refinements and examples added each time.

From the *ahimsa* of Buddha to the *agape* of Jesus, to the moral outrage of Thoreau and Tolstoy against unjust state power, to the syntheses of Mahatma Gandhi and Martin Luther King in the twentieth century, to the work of so many workers for peaceful solutions to the world's problems who were largely unknown before winning the Nobel Peace Prize, and to the daily efforts of millions who will never become famous for their efforts to sustain the world, nonviolence has grown new insights and invented new applications.

It is time to see nonviolence as a paradigm for everyday life, and not simply as a courageous and counterintuitive approach that we are driven to by new crises. Our challenge in the years ahead will be to see in nonviolence a basic ethical and practical foundation for all of life, not just for the one percent in which we feel threatened. The task of extending nonviolence into the other ninety-nine percent is a worthy one for all of us.

About the Authors

IRA G. ZEPP, JR. - The late Ira Zepp (1929-2009) received his doctorate from St. Mary's Seminary and University, and did graduate work in Islam at Hartford Theological Seminary. He studied in India, Mexico, Israel, and Eastern Europe. For 31 years he taught religious studies at McDaniel College (formerly Western Maryland College), and the College's principal teaching award is named for him. A social gospel advocate, he encouraged young people to become involved in the Civil Rights Movement and to work for social justice. He is remembered for saying "To know and not to act, is not to know." He authored many articles and 12 books, two of which are about the thought of Martin Luther King, Jr.

CHARLES E. COLLYER - Charlie Collyer received his doctorate in Psychology from Princeton University in 1976. A professor at the University of Rhode Island for forty years, he was the recipient of several awards for his teaching, and twice served as chair of the Psychology Department. He was a co-founder of the Center for Nonviolence and Peace Studies at URI. With Dr. Pamela Zappardino, he co-directs The Ira and Mary Zepp Center for Nonviolence and Peace Education, a program of the traditional arts organization Common Ground on the Hill, in Westminster MD. Please visit the Center's web page at

http://www.commongroundonthehill.org/zeppcenter.html.
The Zepp Center offers workshops and consultation on
nonviolent problem-solving for organizations and groups of all
kinds. Email address: zeppcenter@gmail.com. Charlie's author
page is www.tryforfurther.com.

WILLIAM A. HOLMES - For 24 years Bill Holmes was the
Senior Minister at Metropolitan Memorial, the National
Methodist Church in Washington DC. Before that, he served
campus-related churches in Dallas, Denton, and Austin, Texas.
He is a graduate of Perkins School of Theology, and did post-
graduate work at Union Theological Seminary in New York,
where he studied with Reinhold Niebuhr and Paul Tillich. He
has served as the Chairman of the Ethics Advisory Committee at
Sibley Memorial Hospital in Washington DC.

BERNARD LAFAYETTE, JR. - Bernard LaFayette, the author
of the Foreword to *Nonviolence: Origins and Outcomes*, was a
Freedom Rider and served as a member of Martin Luther King's
executive staff during the U.S. Civil Rights Movement. He has
been a prominent nonviolence educator ever since Dr. King's
assassination. A Harvard University Ed.D., he is a former
President of his alma mater, American Baptist College in
Nashville, Tennessee. He served as Director of the Center for
Nonviolence and Peace Studies at the University of Rhode
Island and the International Nonviolence Conference Board. He

is currently Distinguished Scholar in Residence at Emory University in Atlanta GA, and Chair of the Southern Christian Leadership Conference.

Endnotes

[1] For examples, see A Force More Powerful, the Public Broadcasting System's series of six short documentaries on successful nonviolent movements for social and political change in India, the United States, Poland, South Africa, Chile, and Denmark. The book of the same name contains chapters on these and several more international examples of nonviolence at work.

[2] For a readable treatment of alternative theories of anger, see Carol Tavris's book Anger: The Misunderstood Emotion (Simon & Schuster).

[3] Some will point out that the Golden Rule is only conditionally nonviolent, because it assumes that a person wants to be treated well. In the case of a person who wishes harm or destruction upon him- or herself, its usefulness as a nonviolent guideline dissolves. For example, in "suicide by police," a person violently attacks police officers because he wants the officers to kill him. However, in this section we ask readers to assume the standard interpretation of the Golden Rule. We should also note that multicultural educators, including our colleague Dr. Pamela Zappardino, prefer a revised, less ego-centric "Platinum Rule," which might be phrased "Treat others as they prefer to be treated." This rule is proactive, giving a guideline for our behavior in advance of knowing what others' behavior will be.

[4] For an excellent treatment of violence from this perspective, see Aaron T. Beck's Prisoners of Hate: The Cognitive Basis of Anger, Hostility, and Violence (Harper Collins).

[5] James Gilligan, M.D., an experienced prison psychiatrist and author of Violence: Reflections on a National Epidemic (Vintage), proposes that all violence is rooted in shame, or disrespect. Gilligan further proposes that love, guilt, fear, and knowledge of alternatives, can serve as brakes on the violence that is triggered by shame. By implication, the occurrence of

violence suggests that these brakes did not work.

[6] The extent to which governments seem to discount the significance of collateral damage when they go to war appalls peace advocates and often radicalizes noncombatants. An important challenge for students of nonviolence is to become more effective at pressing this issue, drawing attention to the unintended consequences of the very neglect of unintended consequences!

[7] Our textbook in this course was Psychology in Perspective, by Tavris and Wade. The five broad perspectives on Psychology presented in this text are: Biological, Learning, Cognitive, and Psychodynamic.

[8] A Force More Powerful is a video series consisting of six short documentaries on nonviolence-inspired movements for social change. A book of the same title by Ackerman and Duvall recounts these and other stories of nonviolence from the 20th Century.

[9] A compact review of several of these is given in Sharon Erickson Nepstad's book Nonviolent Revolutions: Civil Resistance in the Late 20th Century (Oxford, 2011).

[10] The Children, by David Halberstam (Random House, 1998) tells the story of the Nashville sit-in movement through the lives of eight of the young students who led the campaign, one of whom was Bernard LaFayette Jr. The book goes on to trace the involvement of several of these "children" in subsequent events of the Civil Rights Movement, and continues their stories up to the late 1990s. A table of contents for The Children is included in the Kindle e-book A Look Inside David Halberstam's The Children, authored by one of us (Charlie).

[11] Stanley Milgram was a psychologist who became famous for an experiment on obedience to authority. In this experiment, human subjects, who had been told that they were assisting in research on learning, were instructed to deliver ostensibly painful shocks to another person (who was actually an actor). Surprisingly, many subjects continued to obey by increasing the shock level, even when the shocks were

apparently causing injury. The study raised questions of many kinds, but at minimum showed that direct instructions from a person in authority have a powerful influence on behavior.

[12] Tough Guise, a hard-hitting documentary about violence and male socialization by Jackson Katz, was another video seen by this class during the same semester.

[13] Philip Zimbardo, another psychologist, showed that even arbitrarily assigned roles can also strongly shape behavior. In his "prison study" some students played the role of guards and others the role of prisoners in a mock prison. In an account that has become legend in the field of psychology, the study was terminated early because the "guards" went beyond guarding, and began to exhibit cruel and abusive behavior toward their "prisoners."

[14] Walter Wink, a U.S. theologian, uses the term third way to refer to nonviolence as seen in the teachings of Jesus. The first way of responding to an offense or threat would be passivity, or flight. The second would be violent retaliation, or fighting. Nonviolence is a third, more creative alternative in which the opponent and the conflict are engaged deliberately and respectfully. See, for example, Wink's 1998 book The Powers That Be: Theology for a New Millenium, published by Galilee/Doubleday.

[15] A curriculum source book for this approach is the "Leader's Manual": LaFayette, Jr., B., & Jehnsen, D.C. (1995) The Leader's Manual: A structured guide and introduction to Kingian nonviolence: The philosophy and methodology. Galena, OH: Institute for Human Rights and Responsibilities.

[16] Solzhenitsyn, A. (1992) The Gulag Archipelago: 1918-1956. An Experiment in Literary Investigation. Vol. III. New York: Harper/Collins, p. 615.

[17] Ury, W. (1999) Getting to Peace: Transforming Conflict at Home, at work, and in the World. New York: Viking.

[18] King, Jr., M.L. (1963) Strength to Love. Philadelphia: Fortress Press.

[19] Cohen, J.R. & Fiffer, S. (Eds.) (1989). Free at Last: A History of the Civil Rights Movement and Those Who Died in the Struggle. Montgomery AL: Teaching Tolerance.

[20] King, Jr., M. L. (1958). Stride Toward Freedom: The Montgomery Story. San Francisco: Harper.

[21] A more detailed account of this history and of the principles of nonviolence is available in Ira Zepp's work on the Pilgrimage chapter: Smith, K.L. & Zepp, Jr., I.G. (1998) Search for the Beloved Community. Valley Forge PA: Judson; and Zepp, Jr., I.G. (1971) The Social Vision of Martin Luther King, Jr. New York: Carlson.

[22] Gilligan, J. (1996) Violence: Reflections on a National Epidemic. New York: Vintage Books.

[23] Martin Luther King was acutely aware that personal animosities continually threatened both his supporters and those who opposed him. He repeatedly sought a detached and firm but courteous way of prodding both sides to address the issues rather than insulting and spitefully undermining each other.

[24] King, Jr., M. L. (1963) Letter from Birmingham Jail. Chapter 5 (pp. 77-100) in Why We Can't Wait. New York: Harper & Row, p.79.

[25] Daniel Kahneman has drawn attention to the distinction between these two kinds of human cognition in his book Thinking, Fast and Slow (2011) New York: Farrar, Strous and Giroux.

[26] King, Jr., M. L. (1963). Why We Can't Wait. New York: Harper & Row.

[27] Film footage capturing this moment is included in the segment of the video series A Force More Powerful that tells the Nashville story. The segment is title We Were Warriors.

[28] Fisher, R., Ury, W. & Patton, B. (1991) Getting to Yes: Negotiating

Agreement Without Giving In. 2nd ed. New York: Penguin.

[29] King, Jr., M. L. (1963) Why We Can't Wait, p. 79. (Letter from Birmingham Jail).

[30] For example, in current conflicts between the police and youth of color in cities all across the United States, both sides have a "bad apple" problem. That is, the vast majority of police are not trigger-happy, though a few bad apples could be described that way. Likewise, the vast majority of youth are not thugs, although the behavior of a few might lead some people to use that term. Both police and youth are therefore stereotyped in a shallow and misleading, but similar, way. What if this became their common ground? What if a reconciliation is possible in which police use their authority to advocate for the needs of the youth rather than to merely control their behavior through force?

[31] Here is a link to the text of Thoreau's essay:
http://xroads.virginia.edu/~hyper2/thoreau/civil.html

[32] Tolstoy's views are forcefully presented in his book The Kingdom of God is Within You.

[33] For examples, see Chacham, R. (2003), Breaking Ranks: Refusing to Serve in the West Bank and Gaza Strip, New York: Other Press; and Laufer, P. (2006), Mission Rejected: U.S. Soldiers Who Say No to Iraq, White River Junction: Chelsea Green.

[34] Halberstam, D. (1998). The Children. New York, Fawcett, pp. 137-138. See also Collyer, C. E. (2015). A Look Inside David Halberstam's The Children. Kindle ebook.

[35] From Arun Gandhi's pamphlet M. K. Gandhi's Wit and Wisdom, p. 40 (no date). Memphis TN: Gandhi Institute.

[36] From the article Love, law and civil disobedience, in New South, vol. 16, Dec. 1961; quoted in Smith, K. & Zepp Jr., I. G. (1974), Search for the Beloved Community: The thinking of Martin Luther King, Jr. Valley

Forge: Judson.

[37] From the Letter from Birmingham Jail, in MLK's 1963 book Why We Can't Wait, New York: Harper & Row, p. 98.

[38] From Reinhold Niebuhr, Moral Man and Immoral Society (1932), New York: Scribner's, p. 246.

[39] ibid., p. 250.

[40] ibid., p. 252.

[41] From the Letter from Birmingham Jail, in MLK's book Why We Can't Wait (1963), p. 81.

[42] We are grateful to our colleague Frank Gallo for acquainting us with aikido. Frank is a former police officer, a nonviolence trainer, and an aikido master.

[43] Bandura, A., Ross, D., and Ross, S. A. (1961). Transmission of aggression through imitation of aggressive models. Journal of Abnormal and Social Psychology, 63, 575-582.

[44] Johnson, D. W. And Johnson, R. T. (1996). Conflict resolution and peer mediation programs in elementary and secondary schools: A review of the research. Review of Educational Research, Winter 1996, 66, No. 4, 459-506.

[45] Goleman, D. Emotional Intelligence: Why It Can Matter More Than IQ. New York: Bantam, 1995.

[46] Hallak, M. "Nonviolence training program evaluation" (2001). Dissertations and Master's Theses. Paper AAI3025568. http://digitalcommons.uri.edu/dissertations/AAI3025568

[47] Collyer, C. E., Johnson, K. L, de Mesquita, P. B., Palazzo, L. A., & Jordan, D. (2010). Sensitivity to violence measured by ratings of severity increases after nonviolence training. Perceptual & Motor Skills, 110(1), 48-60.

[48] Collyer, C. E., Gallo, F. J., Corey, J., Waters, D., & Boney-McCoy, S.

(2007). Typology of violence derived from ratings of severity and provocation. Perceptual & Motor Skills, 104(2), 637-653.

[49] Collyer, C. E., Brell, A., Moster, A., & Furey, J. (2011). Individual differences in sensitivity to violence. Perceptual & Motor Skills, 113(3), 703-714.

[50] Lipsey, M. W. & Wilson, D. B. (1993). The efficacy of psychological, educational, and behavioral treatment: Confirmation from meta-analysis. American Psychologist, 48, 1181-1209.

[51] Durlak, J. A., Weissberg, R. P., Dymnicki, A. B., Taylor, R. D. & Schellinger, K. B. (2011). The impact of enhancing students' social and emotional learning: A meta-analysis of school-based universal interventions. Child Development, 82(1): 405–432.

[52] Duckworth, A. (2016). Don't grade schools on Grit. New York Times, March 26, 2016.

[53] The description of Just War Theory paraphrases Paul Robinson's in his article titled "Ready to kill but not to die: NATO strategy in Kosovo," International Journal, Autumn 1999.

[54] "Send in a thousand grandmothers"is the first line of the song 1000 Grandmothers, by singer and activist Holly Near.

[55] Nepstad, S. (2011). Nonviolent Revolutions: Civil Resistance in the Late 20th Century (Oxford, 2011).

Made in United States
North Haven, CT
03 September 2024

56922885R00108